The Tao of Objects

SECOND EDITION

Gary Entsminger

M&T Books
A Division of MIS:Press, Inc.
A Subsidiary of Henry Holt and Company, Inc.
115 West 18th Street
New York, New York 10011

Library of Congress Cataloging-in-Publication Data
Entsminger, Gary
 The Tao of objects : a beginners's guide to object-oriented
 programming / Gary Entsminger ; introduction by Bruce Eckel. -- 2nd ed.
   p.   cm.
   Includes index
   ISBN 1-55851-412-0
   1. Object-oriented programming (Computer science)   I. Title.
QA76.64.E58   1995
005.1'1--dc20   95-27
                                                                    CIP

Editor-In-Chief: Paul Farrell
Managing Editor: Cary Sullilvan
Development Editor: Laura Lewin
Copy Editor: Betsy Hardinger
Technical Editor: Jerry Coffey
Production Editor: Stephanie Doyle

for Alison

Contents

Chapter 4: Shaping the System.................. 117

Chapter 5: Dynamic Style 143

Chapter 6: OOP Design in the Real World... 167

Acknowledgments

I'd like to thank a few folks who've supported and advised me, offered suggestions, read the manuscript, provided software, or just plain been helpful during the writing of two editions of this book: Brenda McLaughlin, Linda Comer, Laura Lewin, Jerry Coffey, Zack Urlocker, David Intersimone, Nan Borreson, Karen Giles, Tammy Casey, J.D. Hildebrand, Larry O'Brien, Mike Floyd, Bill Gates, and the cool folks (Kev, bb., Aym, Sonda) at the Rocky Mountain Biological Laboratory. While I'm thinking and writing about objects the snow is falling.

I especially thank Alison Brody, Bruce Eckel, Chester Anderson, and Larry Fogg for the many enlightening hours of discussions while I was designing and writing. I can't wait to see what you do next.

Small portions of this book first appeared in different form in *AI Expert*, *Computer Language*, *Dr. Dobb's Journal*, *Micro Cornucopia*, and *dBASE Informant*.

Bruce Eckel has revised the Introduction for the second edition. Thanks again, Bruce.

I've left Zack Urlocker's Afterword from the first edition intact because it casts an illuminating perspective on the development of OOP since 1990. Thanks again, Zack.

The quotes by Lao-tzu from *The Tao Te Ching* are from the Stephen Mitchell translation (Harper & Row, New York, N.Y., 1988).

The quote by Douglas Hofstadter and Daniel Dennett is from *The Mind's I* (Bantam Books, New York, N.Y., 1981).

The quotes by Fritjof Capra are from *The Tao of Physics* (Shambhala, Berkeley, Calif., 1975).

The quote by Riane Eisler is from *The Chalice and the Blade* (Harper & Row, San Francisco, Calif., 1987).

The inside illustrations are based on photographs by Chester Anderson.

Why This Book Is for You

This book is a guide to objects, object-based software development, and object-oriented programming. It's written for software developers, programmers, and anyone who knows at least a little bit about programming and wants to understand why objects are hot and how they work. In particular, C++, Object Pascal, dBASE, and Visual Basic programmers will learn how to rethink their programs using objects.

The Tao of Objects is friendly—a hands-on book that emphasizes the key advantages of programming with objects. The examples in the book are general enough to be of interest to anyone—and they're fun.

Subjects of particular interest include:

❑ Object-oriented design

❑ Program extension

❑ Modeling systems

❑ Chaos theory and strange attractors

❑ Linked lists

❑ Expert systems

❑ Object-oriented database development

and much more (of course). Most examples are given in C++ and Delphi, the object-oriented successors to C and Pascal. Many examples are given in dBASE for Windows, the object-oriented successor to dBASE, and Visual Basic.

If you're a programmer who wants a gentler introduction to object-oriented programming than a computer manual can provide, or if you're a user wanting to understand what the object hullabaloo is about, this book is for you.

Introduction

Expressing the ideas of object-oriented programming in terms of an Eastern philosophy is a wonderful concept. Gary and I spent many days in the woods and the mountains and many hours on the phone working on this view. Time being what it is (fleeting), I found I didn't have enough, and the book became Gary's. However, I hope I can make additional contributions in this introduction by raising some of the issues I feel are important.

When I explained OOP to my friend Mark (a psychologist), he replied "I don't understand—how else would you do it? How were they doing it before?" I found I was at a loss to describe the old way. I mean, I practiced procedural programming, the structured techniques, and all that, but it never really made sense to me—it never seemed *whole*. In fact, I never took programming very seriously before OOP, probably because it seemed to take too much effort to get the job done. Because I can now think in more powerful terms, I can solve much more complex problems.

One difficulty people have when learning object-oriented programming is finding a way to think about it. Often you hear such unhelpful things as "It's easier for someone who doesn't know how to program to learn OOP than for an experienced programmer" or "You need to unlearn what you know." My personal experience has not supported this. Although thinking about objects is different from thinking about procedural programming, it's different because you're stepping into a larger world, not because everything you know is wrong. This is especially true with hybrid languages such as C++ and Borland Pascal (the underlying programming language in Delphi); you'll see that the ability to create user-defined data types isn't such a radical idea, because you use data types so much that you usually don't even think about them. However, it does tend to highlight the limitations of the built-in types and (to my mind) the relative primitiveness of what we've been using as programming languages so far. Once you begin using an object-oriented language, it's hard to go back.

History and Concepts

When the Simula language was developed in Scandinavia in the late sixties, its designers were trying to make the process of simulation easier (hence the name). Simulations always seem to involve a group of things— customers in line in a bank, molecules of air, migrating animals—in short, a lot of objects. An object knows things about itself: It has an internal state, or characteristics. It can also do things: It has external operations, or behaviors. It turns out that this also describes the data types built into a programming language. It's just that the data types cannot express the features necessary to model a real-world system.

Existing languages engendered very messy code when a simulation was created because their types were so limited. It looked as if the only way to make simulation easy was to change the language so that the programmer could add new types of data. This abstract data typing is a fundamental concept in object-oriented programming. Abstract data types work almost exactly like built-in types: You can create variables of a type (called *objects* or *instances* in object-oriented parlance) and manipulate those variables (called *sending messages*; you send a message and the object figures out what to do with it).

The language designers also discovered that a type does more than describe the constraints on a set of objects; it also has a relationship with other types. Two types can have characteristics and behaviors in common, but one type may contain more characteristics than another and may also handle more messages (or may handle them differently). Inheritance was developed to express this relationship between types. It uses the concept of base types and derived types. A base type has all the characteristics and behaviors that are shared among the types derived from it. You create a base type to represent the core of your ideas about the objects in your system. From it, you derive other types to express the different ways in which that core can be realized.

For example, a garbage-recycling machine sorts pieces of garbage. The base type is garbage, and each piece of garbage has a weight, a value, and so on and can be shredded, melted, or decomposed. From this, we derive specific types of garbage that may have additional characteristics (a bottle has a color) or behaviors (an aluminum can may be crushed, a steel can is magnetic). In addition, some behaviors may be different (the value of paper depends on its type and condition). Using inheritance, you can build a type hierarchy that expresses the problem you're trying to solve in terms of its types.

Casting the solution in the same terms as the problem is tremendously beneficial because you don't need a lot of intermediate models (used with procedural languages for large problems) to get from a description of the problem to a description of the solution; in pre–object oriented languages the solution was inevitably described in terms of computers. With objects, the type hierarchy is the primary model, so you go directly from the description of the system in the real world to the description of the system in code. Indeed, one of the difficulties people have with object-oriented design is that it's too simple to get from the beginning to the end. A mind trained to look for complex solutions is often stumped by this simplicity, and when I say, "The types are the primary model, and the best representation for the types is the code," most people don't believe me (at first).

Once you've modeled your problem as a set of types, writing the code becomes remarkably simple; it's mostly a matter of creating objects and sending messages to them. The objects take care of the details and ensure their own integrity.

When dealing with type hierarchies, you often want to treat an object not as the specific type that it is but instead as a member of its base type. This allows you to write code that doesn't depend on specific types. For instance, the now-classic "shape" example has functions that manipulate generic shapes without respect to whether they're circles, squares, triangles, and so on. Because all shapes can be drawn, erased, and moved, these functions simply send a message to a shape object; they don't worry about how the object copes with the message.

Such code is unaffected by the addition of new types, which is the most common way to extend an object-oriented program to handle new situations. For example, you can derive a new subtype of shape called pentagon without modifying the functions that deal only with generic shapes. The ability to extend a program easily by deriving new subtypes is important because it greatly reduces the cost of software maintenance (the so-called software crisis was caused by the observation that software was costing more than people thought it ought to).

There's a problem, however, with attempting to treat derived-type objects as their generic base types (circles as shapes, bicycles as vehicles, cormorants as birds). If a function is going to tell a generic shape to draw itself, or a generic vehicle to steer, or a generic bird to fly, the compiler cannot know at compile time precisely what piece of code will be executed. That's the point—when the message is sent, the programmer doesn't *want* to know what piece of code will be executed; the function can be equally applied to a circle, a square, or a triangle, and the object will execute the proper code depending on its specific type. If you add a new subtype, the code it executes can be different without changes to the function. If the compiler cannot know precisely what piece of code is executed, what does it do?

The answer is the primary twist in object-oriented programming: The compiler cannot make a function call in the traditional sense. The function call generated by a non-OOP compiler causes what is called *early binding*, a term you may not have heard before because you've never thought about it any other way. It means that the compiler generates a call to a specific function name, and the linker resolves that call to an absolute address of the code to be executed. In OOP, the program cannot determine the address of the code until run time, so some other scheme is necessary when a message is sent to a generic object.

To solve the problem, object-oriented languages use the concept of *late binding*. When you send a message to an object, the code being called isn't determined until run time. The compiler *does* ensure that the function exists and performs type checking on the arguments and return value (a language in which this isn't true is called *weakly typed*), but the compiler doesn't know the exact code to execute.

To perform late binding, the compiler inserts a special bit of code in lieu of the absolute call. This code calculates the address of the code to execute using a pointer stored in the object itself. This pointer, called the *VPTR* in C++ and the *VMT pointer* in Borland Pascal (Delphi), points to a table of function addresses. These are the addresses of all the functions in this generic base type that have late-binding properties. Because each object contains its own pointer, it can behave differently according to the contents of that pointer. Thus, when you send a message to an object, the object actually does figure out what to do with that message.

Late binding requires extra code to calculate the function address and a little bit of extra time in which to calculate it. Some programmers (especially C programmers, who are notorious for their fanatical views on efficiency) may object to this overhead. Some object-oriented languages force late binding for all functions, but in the spirit of C and Pascal you have a choice. You state that you want a function to have the flexibility of late-binding properties using the keyword `virtual` in C++ and Borland Pascal (Delphi); without the keyword, slightly more efficient early binding is performed.

You don't need to understand the meaning of `virtual` to use it, but you can't do object-oriented programming in these languages without it. It's the key to the kingdom; once you understand how to use virtual functions, you'll understand OOP (which, although it may be a silly-sounding acronym, is useful in part because it keeps us humble). You'll find further illumination about `virtual` in the pages of this book.

Templates and Exception Handling

Since the first edition of this book, two major features have been added to the C++ language: templates and exception handling. An exception-handling mechanism very similar to the C++ model was also added to Delphi. Although exception handling encompasses more than this book chose to bite off, the template feature is exploited in several of the C++ examples. They're both important features, and you should be aware of them.

It's fairly easy to reuse code in C++ and Delphi. You can use inheritance to express an *is-a* relationship (a circle *is-a* type of shape, a car *is-a* type of vehicle). You can also use *composition* to express a *has-a* relationship; you simply stick an object of an existing type inside your new type (a car *has-a* motor, wheel, window, etc.). However, both approaches reuse *object* code—they just call compiled functions from the existing classes. Sometimes that's not enough. In particular, the concept of *container classes* (objects that hold other objects—you use these instead of primitive arrays) cries out to reuse *source* code, because it's very important for the container to know the exact type it's holding or, more likely, holding a pointer to. The reuse of source code is achieved in C++ (but not in Delphi) with the *template* feature. Fortunately, you don't have to understand it to use it; many libraries are appearing now that use templates (including the Standard C++ library). The use of these libraries is amazingly simple (as you'll see in the C++ examples in this book that use the `list` class template), so now the use of a container class (which encompasses all those structures and algorithms you may not remember from your data structures course) becomes virtually effortless.

The true goal of OOP is not to foist upon you some new, "correct" way of thinking about programming. Its basis is economic: We want to create and maintain large, robust programs more quickly and easily and with fewer programmers than ever before. All the features discussed so far help you build such programs. But something is always overlooked when creating programs: errors. It's as if we think, "errors won't happen to me." This is understandable, because error-handling schemes have never been particularly easy or useful. In fact, if you think about it, traditional error-handling schemes are abysmal: To properly check for errors you'd have to surround *every single function call* with error-checking code. No wonder people don't do it: It requires a ton of extra code and it's very distracting—you're trying to figure out what to do to solve your problem, and you must always be thinking about errors.

In C++ and Delphi, the error problem is solved using *exception handling*. This allows you to write the code that you *want* to happen, as if errors won't occur (admit it—this is the way you've been writing most of your code anyway!). In a separate section, you write *handlers*, one handler for each type of error that may occur. This not only separates the code that normally executes from the error code, but it also reduces the amount of error-handling code you must write because you need only one handler for a particular error regardless of how many functions you call that may generate that error.

There are two other important features in exception handling: First, all objects will be properly cleaned up. An object in C++ and Delphi can be a complicated entity that requires some sort of cleanup when it is destroyed. The exception-handling mechanism guarantees this cleanup will occur. Secondly, with exception handling, errors cannot be ignored. Somewhere there must exist a handler for every possible error (even if it's a default handler). If an exception is "thrown," the run-time mechanism searches for a handler until it finds a match. If it can't find a handler, it's considered a program bug. Thus you have a guarantee (well, almost— there are no guarantees in life, the Tao, or programming) that an error cannot be ignored. This is especially important when you're building and using libraries.

Exception handling is not an object-oriented feature. Although it's very helpful to have objects in conjunction with exception handling (a different type of object represents each type of error), exception handling is orthogonal to OOP. In fact, the first exception-handling mechanisms were implemented in the '60s, in operating systems rather than in programming languages. The Win32 operating systems (including Windows NT and Windows 95) have an exception-handling mechanism built in; each programming language for those platforms may have different models to implement exceptions—Win32 C compilers, for example, use a function-based exception-handling syntax. The C++ model of exception handling follows ADA's exceptions, and Delphi's syntax follows C++'s.

Code Reuse

An issue that is often raised in object-oriented programming is code reuse. Many programmers find this confusing because they feel code reuse is already embodied in named subroutines (which we call *functions* in C++

and Pascal, although Pascal uses an additional subtype of *function* called a *procedure*). Since calling a function in more than one place reuses the code in that function, isn't that code reuse?

Although the answer to this may be "yes" in a discussion of pre–object-oriented languages, OOP takes it much further. Code reuse in object-oriented programming means type reuse. You reuse a type in two situations: when it satisfies your needs in the form it's in and when you can make it satisfy your needs with small additions or modifications. The beauty of the second case is that you can make changes without touching the original code (a statement that at first sounds contradictory) using inheritance.

If you want to create a new type and you have one that does most of what you need, you can inherit the existing type into the new one, add new data and functions, and change the meaning of existing functions. This is a powerful tool because it lets you make modifications and improvements without touching (or breaking) existing code. Any bugs that show up are automatically isolated to the new code. Code reuse in an object-oriented language is thus a fundamentally different and more useful concept than it is in procedural languages; it increases both your power and your flexibility.

Language Extensibility

Because we're effectively extending the language by creating new data types that the compiler treats as built-in types, the specter of the extensible language rears its head. Although some extensible languages such as Forth are still popular in small circles, they are generally considered to be failures as general-purpose languages. That's because of the propensity of programmers to create their own languages, which is exactly what an extensible language is intended for. In a sense, it has many similarities to object-oriented programming because you modify an extensible language until it fits the problem you're trying to solve, and you add types to an OOP environment until they model the problem you're trying to solve.

The difficulty with extensible languages is that code written in a programmer's own version of that language tends to be write-only. Object-oriented languages don't suffer from this problem for two reasons.

First, extensible languages never made a clear distinction between the base language and the programmer's extensions to the language. Although some of these languages tried to delineate the core of the language (and thus what you could expect to be there), agreement was difficult to reach, in part because there was never a good reason to draw the line on language extensions. In addition, you can change the basic meaning of almost anything in an extensible language such as Forth, so you don't necessarily know whether your environment has a function; if that function exists, you don't necessarily know what it does. Thus, these sorts of languages produce a maintenance nightmare.

C++ and Borland Pascal (Delphi) are hybrid OOP languages, which means that they were created from existing languages. The existing languages have a distinct set of built-in types, although the programmers who use "pure" OOP languages such as Smalltalk observe that the built-in types suffer from inadequacies absent in "real" OOP types; this can be rectified with small overhead by creating new types from the built-in types. The compiler knows only about the built-in types until you tell it about the user-defined types you want to use. Thus, there's a clear line between the core of the language—what's built into the compiler—and an extension (always added at compile time). Neither the programmer nor the reader of the code will ever have any doubt where this line is. Pure languages such as Smalltalk don't have this distinction, and the two primary flavors of Smalltalk differ in the types available in the basic system. (This system is notably vast; one of the obstacles to learning Smalltalk is its large library of types. The large library is also its primary strength.)

Second, the extensions in OOP languages are only in terms of types—and not in the fundamental control structures and operators—and the compiler checks to make sure that instances of these types are used properly. Thus, you don't have the "shifting-sands" approach seen in extensible languages—the rules for type extension are very clear and are enforced by the compiler.

The bottom line is accountability—you always know how to find out what a piece of code means in an OOP language, whereas *anything* can be modified and changed in an extensible language without any sort of audit trail. The reader of the code in an extensible language cannot be certain what the code means because it depends on the extended version of the language it's running on.

Advantages of Hybrid Languages

A hybrid OOP language has the disadvantage that its built-in types may behave slightly differently from user-defined types. In addition, some programmers complain about the dearth of user-defined types that come with a programming environment (in comparison to Smalltalk, which has many types). This limitation is being rectified as standards develop—for example, the Standard C++ library is quite diverse and a significant foundation for other library vendors. However, languages such as C++ and Borland Pascal (Delphi) are intended to support many large and diverse libraries and not to be restricted to libraries that they provide.

One might find fault with hybrid OOP languages, but certain features are undeniable advantages. First and foremost is the learning curve. Essentially, programmers who are versed in the non–object-oriented versions of the language can begin using the object-oriented versions immediately, albeit without using any of the new features. Although it may be theoretically convenient to say, "Throw away everything you know and learn it the right way," it's hardly practical. This is seen in the tremendous migration of C programmers to C++.

Not only is it comfortable for programmers who aren't ready for the full force of OOP, but learning the new OOP features in the context of a familiar language also seems much easier than learning an entirely new language and new concepts at the same time. The differences between the old and new ways of thinking are clear, so programmers know when they're venturing into new territory. The final comfort is that they know they can always go back to the old style.

In a hybrid language, not everything needs to be an object. Everything in a pure object-oriented language is an object, even the type definitions. This is the object-oriented philosophy taken to the extreme. Although it has a purist appeal, it isn't always practical. Sometimes you need a function or an ordinary chunk of memory; to be arbitrarily forced to make everything an object can be an unwieldy constraint.

Another important advantage of hybrid OOP languages is that large bodies of legacy code can still be used. C++ is designed to compile Standard C code with few or no changes, and Delphi is designed to compile previous Borland Pascal with minimal changes. Thus, you can move to OOP without losing previous work.

Philosophical Differences

This book attempts to highlight the similarities between C++ and Borland Pascal (Delphi), but I think it's also helpful to note the differences and evaluate their differing philosophies.

The Standard C language has, by necessity, been a compromise between the many divergent implementations of the C language that propagated as a result of the original, incompletely specified language. Although the ANSI C committee recognized the problems and holes in the resulting language, they didn't feel they could fill those holes without breaking significant amounts of existing code.

C++ has always had a single definition, created by its inventor, Bjarne Stroustrup. The definition is verified and formalized by the actions of the ANSI/ISO C++ committee, but there has never been the divergence experienced by C; the definition and original implementation came from Stroustrup and company at AT&T and has gone almost directly to the ANSI/ISO C++ committee. Although C++ is designed to compile as much existing C code as possible without change, it is also designed to produce very large systems, and this requires more strict support for safety. Thus, holes in the C language were filled so that the compiler could catch errors that would otherwise go unnoticed. Closing these holes has restricted the C code that can be compiled. This is a safer, slightly smaller subset of existing C code, and C programmers will notice small differences in the language. I feel that most people will see these differences as improvements, but they will definitely notice that C++ is not exactly C.

In addition, basic philosophies have been adhered to in the design of C++ that give a different feel to the language—in particular, the idea that you should never have uninitialized variables in a program. You can define variables at any point in a scope and wait until you have all the necessary information before defining the variable. Also, the compiler automatically generates calls to constructors (special functions that initialize a variable). The constructors ensure that both the data members and the VPTR are initialized. Philosophies such as this have a definite impact on the way you program.

In Borland Pascal (Delphi), the design philosophy was very different. The intent was to leave the core language absolutely unchanged and make sure that users who didn't want to know about OOP were unaffected by the additions to the language. No programs need to be modified because of the changes. This approach is insightful but has distinctly different goals. Because type checking in Pascal was already quite strong, no major holes remain to be closed in that area. However, Pascal would need to be written and compiled much differently to ensure initialized variables. The VAR section makes it very difficult to define and initialize variables at any point in a block and to call constructors at the point of definition; the programmer must call them explicitly at a later point. If they're forgotten, the initialization won't take place. This is particularly bad if the variable contains a VMT pointer.

The Borland Pascal (Delphi) programmer must be vigilant. It's unfortunate, but I don't see how it could have been circumvented without changing the language so significantly that it would have violated the goal of full code compatibility.

In this book, the differences are pointed out only when it's necessary (as in the need to explicitly call constructors in Pascal). The differences don't influence the effectiveness of the basic OOP ideas in either language.

Design

The analogy of the Tao with object-oriented programming is most obvious when you're making a first cut at a problem or thinking about OOP design. Programmers have become so accustomed to thinking in terms of complexity—complexity of the hardware, complexity in the design process, complexity in the implementation, and complexity when modeling and documenting a system—that their first reaction to OOP is often something like, "Where are the bits and bytes and `for` loops?" There's great resistance when you're presented with code that describes the system you're trying to solve rather than the system in which you're trying to solve it.

In addition, we have somehow been taught that starting to program before solving the problem on paper is heresy. This attitude is understandable; we've all seen the spaghetti code created by programmers who dove in without any plan at all. Coding by the seat of your pants works with small problems but stops working when you cross a mysterious size boundary. However, the concept of planning is usually taken to the opposite, impractical extreme. Everyone talks about it, but in the end it appears to require too much time, so people go back to programming by the seat of their pants. In addition, the meaning of "small" when applied to programming problems certainly changes depending on the tools available to manage complexity; one programmer dashing off a few lines of C++ code is the equivalent of man-months of machine language programmer time in the '50s. The amount and type of planning must be adjusted downward as the programming tools become more powerful. This promotes a strong argument that methods should be less complicated and require less time and effort for OOP than for procedural languages.

Too much planning is impractical, anyway—we learn through experimentation, not by doing thought examples as the Greeks were wont to do with their physics. One of the benefits of OOP is that user-defined data types tend to partition a program into stable pieces; procedural programming requires programmer discipline to prevent an unstable design, whereas OOP supports a tendency toward increasing stability. Parts of the program that are unstable won't affect parts that are, because user-defined data types focus behaviors of the program in tightly coupled areas of code. The two fundamental design guidelines of programming—high coupling and low cohesion—are still valid but must be applied (like everything else in OOP) to entire types rather than to individual functions.

In the philosophy of the Tao, the focus is on the path rather than the destination, the process rather than the goal. The same, I think, is true of OOP design and problem-solving. If you focus on a particular implementation, you may tie yourself to a solution that you later find to be unworkable; you may not want to end up where you originally thought you did. Focusing more on the goal than on the path may mean that you'll end up in the wrong place because you ignored valuable information—you already had all those design documents, and your mind was made up. The way of the Tao is to let the path show you the way. Applying this philosophy to object-oriented programming means letting the process of solving the problem show you what the objects should be and what they should look like.

The bulk of Chapter 7 (on design) is derived from notes I made while musing about the design problem in OOP versus structured techniques. (Like all zealots, I couldn't understand why all programmers didn't flock to this so obviously *correct* way of developing programs; only later did I figure out that programmers like to program, not write seven different types of documentation.) I keep coming to the conclusion that the best model for the program is the program itself. Every time I try to come up with a different representation, I seem to end up with something more complicated than just writing down the type declarations.

That's why I emphasize that the best approach for object-oriented programmers is to start writing down type declarations and fill out from there. Don't worry if you don't know everything when you start creating the types; as you develop the system, you'll see the answers and the details will sort themselves out. This is very different from the idea that you must know everything before you write a single line of code, but it's one of the reasons OOP is so powerful—it's more reflective and supportive of the way programmers actually do things (they write code).

Back and Forth

One of the great things that's happening because of the almost frightening success of C++ is that the language model adopted for C++ is being studied and adapted in other languages that are adding object-oriented extensions. Because of this, the knowledge acquired in the understanding of C++ is becoming portable to other languages; object-oriented extensions are being considered or have been added to languages such as Ada, FORTRAN, COBOL, and PROLOG. A language in which this is especially useful is Borland Delphi.

The underlying Pascal language has been "objectified" over the last few years, and it closely follows the C++ model, often even down to the keywords. So as a C++ programmer, you find the familiar data protection, constructors/destructors, exception handling, virtual keyword, references, and so on, without a lot of the confusing extra features from C++ such as operator overloading. The syntax is similar, and the form of the code is immediately recognizable so that you put all the elements in the same place—a `begin` goes in the same spot as you'd put a { in C++, and so on. This means that a programmer can be reasonably fluent in both without much strain. Although I'm a huge fan of C++ and the code-generation tools and class libraries that have been flowing from vendors at an astounding rate, I'm a bigger fan of the most economical solution, and for many Windows programmers the value of Delphi as a rapid Windows development tool should not be ignored. For a programmer, the development of all these competing tools is clearly a winning situation no matter where you look.

Buying In

Programmers often feel that someone is trying to sell them something. There are the traditional folks who are simply trying to make money, but the more persistent and zealous ones are those who try to get "mind share." Choosing a language involves both, so the efforts heat up even more.

More intellectually sophisticated programming languages than C++ and Delphi certainly exist, and some languages are easier to learn; both types have been pushed as "better." As effective as the sell jobs have been, we aren't selling soap here—programmers are a sophisticated audience, and a suspicious one. It doesn't take long for negative reviews to get back to the pack, and a language that once seemed promising becomes mediocre or, worse, laughable. You can't hide for long the fact that a language has been created by someone with a particular bent or background, an axe to grind, or a single good idea. Programmers will tolerate some flaws and limitations in a new language, but not too many, and not if the flaws are capricious, gratuitous, or myopic.

Programmers often switch to OOP when offered C++ and Delphi even if they resisted earlier languages, because that feeling of "rightness" has been struck: It's not too different, the learning time of the programmer has not been considered unimportant in favor of the "proper" language purity, and those programmers who value such issues as efficiency, ROMability, real time, and robustness have not been dismissed. As much as possible, the practical issues as well as the desire for conceptual purity have been mixed together in these languages, and programmers haven't taken long to see that it's (finally) the right compromise—until the next great concept in computer science shows up (multineural nonlinear persistent room-temperature-superconducting C++, anyone?).

Programmers work out a model in their heads of how things work and have some trouble dislodging that model once they've tested it and come to believe in it. This prevents them from making big mistakes, such as switching to a language that's too limited for their needs, but it also significantly slows down the shift to a more powerful way of thinking. When I asked Andrew Koenig (editor of the ANSI/ISO C++ document) to name the most frequently encountered problem among people learning OOP, he said it was the belief that a programming language is for manipulating pieces of memory rather than for manipulating concepts.

A language provides an interface between us and some machine-implemented agents. A good language attempts to insulate us, as much as possible, from the details and limitations of the particular agents (without preventing us from getting our work done). As long as we persist in doing assembly-language programming in whatever high-level language we're using, we'll be constrained to solving a small subset of problems. The really big problems are solved by dealing with the concepts, not an intermediate representation of the concepts (chunks of memory, data-flow diagrams, structure charts, and so on).

OOP languages *support* this way of thinking about problems, and languages such as Smalltalk may even *force* you to think this way (but require the effort of learning an entirely foreign language and set of rules). In C++ and Borland Delphi, you aren't forced. As simple and optional as the language extensions may seem, remember that they are only support for OOP and won't make your programs better unless you can eventually shift your thinking from bytes to concepts. This book should help you make that shift.

Bruce Eckel
first edition: December 1990
second edition: October 1994

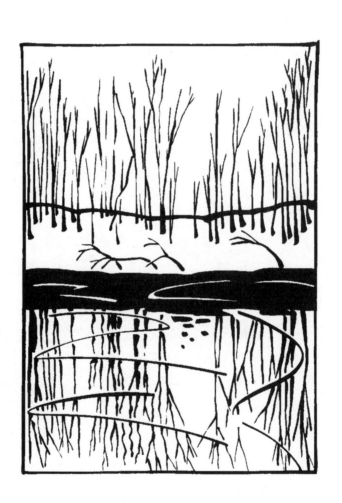

Chapter
One

Great Journeys, Single Steps

The soft overcomes the hard; the gentle overcomes the rigid.
Everyone knows this is true, but few can put it into practice.

—Lao-tzu

What makes you you, and what are your boundaries?
—Douglas R. Hofstadter and Daniel C. Dennett

Ancient Chinese philosophers believed in a unifying reality called the *Tao* (pronounced "dow"). These philosophers of the Way emphasized that the world is impermanent and dynamic, not static. To realize this flow (of things, of reality) is to acquire peace.

The objects that compose the world are reflections of processes—in flux and ever-changing. Thus, the perception that we can capture or model an object's essence is illusory; we can capture a bit of anything for only a short while.

A computer program, too, is a process—a tool, a way to model, capture, or simulate part of the world, but traditionally a static concept. Structured programming techniques, although important and useful, don't make it easy to model the world or to modify models once they're built.

Object-based design and object-oriented programming (OOP) are major attempts at making the design, development, and use of programs more dynamic. Using OOP techniques, you can create programs that are adaptive. You can create and destroy complex processes at compile time and run time, and you can design programs that can evolve.

When I wrote the first edition of this book in 1990, few applications and few application development systems were object-based. Not so now. For example, the most powerful database applications treat almost everything within their environments as objects. Disk files, tables, reports, queries, folders, scripts, and libraries are all objects. One mainstream database system, dBASE for Windows, has gone a step further. dBASE for Windows 5.0 includes object-oriented programming capability and a visual form design "expert" that creates object-oriented code automatically. Some general-purpose development applications, such as Microsoft's Visual Basic and Borland's Delphi, are also object-based and (to somewhat different degrees) object-oriented.

In an object-based system, users implicitly, and programmers explicitly, treat all the existing components of a system as objects. Each time you create a new table, form, or application you create an instance (an object) of the table, form, or application based on an existing table, form, or application class. In the Tao's terms, a *class* is a user-defined type or prototype that you use to create specific objects based on the class. An instance (or variable) of a class is an *object*.

This distinction between class and object is important. It might help you to understand this distinction if you consider the relationship between cookies and a cookie cutter. The cookie cutter is a class. It defines the shape and size of cookies. The cookies are objects.

Object-based and object-oriented systems differ in that an object-based system doesn't let you use a programming language (or design tool) to create your own classes. In an object-based system you create instances of existing classes. Usually you can use an object as is or modify its properties. However, in object-oriented systems—such as C++, Smalltalk, Delphi, and dBASE for Windows—you can derive new objects from existing classes of objects, modify and manipulate those objects, and create brand new classes of objects as well.

Object-oriented programming adds three key features—encapsulation, inheritance, and polymorphism—to structured programming. These features let you more clearly envision a program as a dynamic process and plan for its inevitable evolution. Whereas most programming systems force you to accept a static model of the world as the best it can do, object-oriented programming systems assume that the world and the programs you use to model it will change and evolve.

Putting data and the operations to manipulate data together is called *encapsulation.* Or, more technically, encapsulation separates the interface of an application from the implementation. The interface is what users see. The implementation is visible to programmers, but these details are private and hidden from users. You might say that a class protects data.

Deriving new classes of objects from existing classes is called *inheritance.* You use this powerful technique to create hierarchical classes of objects. Hierarchies are useful for organizing many kinds of information.

The new classes you derive can retain the properties and behaviors of their superclass or can reimplement some or all behaviors. A subclass can't remove an existing property of its superclass but can change the default values of these properties. For example, a base class `shapes` can have a behavior (or *method*) `draw`. A new derived shape, or subclass, `rectangle`, can reimplement `draw` as it sees fit. This is *polymorphism*.

Object-oriented programming is a new way to write programs and to relate programs to the world. You create objects in programs that are self-contained, reusable, modifiable and easily managed (because data and the code to manipulate these data elements are in one place). OOP is a method and a natural philosophy. Because you're already familiar with objects in the world and organize information in the world hierarchically, your programs and designs should reflect your knowledge. In the world, you use the same name to "do" different things. Why not in your programs.

Because objects can be reused and modified, programmers and developers don't have to have all the answers to a problem at the beginning of the development cycle. Information and techniques can change as subclasses evolve. You can alter any derived class without necessarily changing other components of the system. You can fix the broken parts without disrupting the working ones. Everyone can be more productive and a bit more sane.

About This Book

This book consists of:

❏ Seven chapters containing short examples in C++, Delphi (an object-oriented Pascal-based language), Visual Basic, and dBASE for Windows

❏ A glossary

❏ A reference list of books and journals to help you pursue object-oriented programming

❏ An index.

Chapters 1–5 and Chapter 7 are completely revised for this edition, incorporating the major changes that have occurred in OOP between 1990 and 1995.

Chapters 1 and 2 introduce classes, objects, and object orientation. They focus on the general features that compose object-oriented languages. Chapters 3, 4, and 5 refine the concepts introduced in those chapters. Chapter 6, entirely new for the second edition, explores object-oriented database programming using dBASE for Windows and Visual Basic. Chapter 7 discusses the implications of object-oriented programming and describes a method for incorporating OOP techniques in applications programming.

The many examples in this book are in C++, Delphi, dBASE for Windows, and Visual Basic whenever appropriate. I try to use language that's consistent with the AT&T C++ 2.1 specification (the primary base document for the ANSI C++ committee), the ANSI C specification, and the Borland C++, Microsoft C++, Delphi, dBASE for Windows, and Visual Basic manuals.

Chaos and strange attractors, phase and state spaces, templates, agents (secret and otherwise), spreadsheets, expert systems, databases, and intelligent system design are a few of the ideas you'll explore. If the world you're trying to model in your programs is dynamic, I think you'll enjoy using object-oriented programming techniques to develop your own ideas. I do.

Languages: Beginning with C++ and Delphi

Although C++ and Delphi (in the form of its ancestor Turbo Pascal) weren't the first object-oriented languages, they are two of the most important and most influential. In particular, C++ represents the "standard" hybrid OOP language. This Tao begins here, with C++, and to a slightly lesser extent, Delphi, as reference points. You'll soon discover that approaches to design and programming in general—and to the way OOP should be implemented—differ. One goal of this book is to illuminate these differences.

For example, C++ and Delphi use different terms to represent similar concepts:

CONCEPT	C++	DELPHI
data structure	struct	record
user-defined type	class	class (object type)
variable of user-defined type	object	instance (object)
data field	member	property, field
behavior	member function, method	method

> **Note:** Since the first edition of *The Tao of Objects* in 1990, Delphi has superseded Turbo Pascal, its object-oriented ancestor, in both language and implementation, moving closer to C++ in many OOP respects.

Some languages, such as Smalltalk, Actor, and Eiffel, effectively treat everything as objects. We sometimes call these languages *pure*. Others, such as C++ and Delphi—the *hybrids* —extend structured languages to handle classes and objects. In hybrid languages you have the option of using classes and objects, but you don't have to.

True to the spirit of the Tao, there are many other OOP paths to choose from. Each path takes a slightly different approach to the same goal: a better way to create software. The pure, or completely object-oriented, languages treat everything according to the same principles. This makes the languages consistent but sometimes a bit awkward, especially for those of us who have been using traditional languages such as C, Basic, and Pascal.

For example, in Smalltalk, a pure OOP language, even simple code such as adding numbers is considered object-oriented. To add a number to a number (simple code), you send a plus message to number objects. Or consider a traditional `if` statement. In Smalltalk, this is written as an `IfTrue` message to a `Condition` object that evaluates to true or false.

Languages such as Actor and Eiffel are more understandable to traditional programmers. These languages use enough "syntactic sugar," or embellishments, to make them accessible to those familiar with C or Pascal. Yet they retain the elegance and consistency of a completely object-oriented environment.

You can use any of these languages (and others) to explore the world of object-oriented programming. But if you're a C or Pascal programmer, C++ and Delphi are excellent ways to begin learning about OOP. If you're strictly a database programmer, try dBASE for Windows, which includes a complete OOP implementation.

Because I assume that you know how to program in some language, such as C, Pascal, or Basic, I won't spend time going over basic programming concepts. Instead, I'll focus on the object-based and object-oriented aspects of modern programming.

Object orientation will undoubtedly bend your mind a little, but if you're open-minded, the bending will be more fun than difficult.

Objects and Actions

The world consists of objects and actions. In our human languages we typically use sentences to relate information about objects. A sentence is an object, and it's composed of objects. Nouns or pronouns are the subjects or topics of sentences. And nouns and pronouns can have characteristics or properties:

> A red ball.
>
> A swooping raven.

Red and *swooping* are descriptive properties.

> Actions (or verbs) express or exhibit behavior:
>
> > The wind blows.
> >
> > A bird sings.
> >
> > A girl swings.
> >
> > A window opens.

Noun and verb together compose a simple sentence, an object. You could describe this base sentence class as follows in pseudocode:

```
Class Sentence {
      Subject:    Noun or pronoun;
      Action:     Verb;
};
```

You can also derive new classes of sentences, for example a Noun + adjective sentence. Call this sentence `NounPSentence` (for NounPhraseSentence):

```
Class NounPSentence {
      Subject: Noun or pronoun;
      Prop1: Adjective;
      Action:Verb;
};
```

This kind of sentence has all the characteristics and behaviors of `Sentence`, and in addition the additonal property, `Prop1`.

Make as many instances (objects) of either sentence as you like, adding new properties and behaviors as you create the sentences. In OOP terms, data (the noun phrase of the sentence) are the properties of an object, and methods (functions or procedures or the verb phrase of the sentence) are its behaviors.

An object-oriented programming language encapsulates an object's characteristics and behaviors within a single block of source code. Putting properties and behaviors in one place makes good sense; it's safer and more convenient.

Robust object-oriented programming languages, such as C++, Delphi, and dBASE for Windows, give programmers the power to create their own classes (sometimes called *user-defined types*), which the compiler treats just like built-in types. You build complex types (*subclasses*) from simpler ones (*superclasses*) that share properties and behaviors.

But programmers have been creating new types all along—by collecting variables into `structs` (in C), `records` (in Pascal), and `types` (in Basic). The only difference is that the functions to manipulate these types have been ordinary ones, scattered about a program and not contained within a single structure with data.

The new *class* designation looks a lot like its data-only counterpart (`struct`, `record`, etc.), but it's self-contained: Data and the procedures to manipulate the data are encapsulated in one package.

> **Note:** Turbo Pascal, which I discussed in the first edition of this book, does not use the now-standard class designation. In TP, object type = class. Delphi uses the standard class designation. This edition of *The Tao of Objects* uses the Delphi class designation.

In C++, you might declare a `struct` like this:

```
struct aStruct {
char Name[10];
int X,Y;
};
```

In Delphi, you could declare a `record` like this:

```
type
        record1 = aRecord;
        aRecord = record
            Name : string;
            X,Y : integer;
        end;
```

In C++, you can declare a `class` like this:

```
class aClass {
public:
        Int X,Y;
        void doSomethingWithXandY();
};
```

`Public` is a keyword meaning "anyone can use it." Things that aren't public can be accessed only by class methods.

You define a variable of type `aClass` like this:

```
aClass classvar;
```

In Delphi, you can define a new form class like this:

```
type
        FormClass 1= class (Tform)
        public
            X,Y : integer;
            procedure doSomethingWithXandY;
end;
```

A variable of type `FormClass1` looks like this:

```
var
        ThisForm: FormClass1;
```

X and Y are properties, and `doSomethingWithXandY` is a method for manipulating an object of the class.

To access the members of a specific object, you use exactly the same selection operators available for `structs` in C and `records` in Pascal—"." for variables and "->" for pointers to variables in C++:

```
cv.X = 2;
cv.doSomethingWithXandY();        /* call  method! */
cp->x = 2;
cp->doSomethingWithXandY();
```

and "." or a *with* statement in Delphi:

```
ThisForm.X := 2;
ThisForm..doSomethingWithXandY;          {* call method! *}

With ThisForm do
  begin
      X:= 2;
      Y:= 4;
      doSomethingWithXandY;
  end;
```

Notice that you don't have to pass X and Y to `doSomethingWithXandY`; an object's methods already know about its properties because they're contained within the same type. They share a local scope. Everything in a class is shared. It's like a small town—everyone knows about everyone else within the limits.

This combining of data and code in one class is an important extension of C++ translation units (source-code files) and Delphi units. (I'll refer to both simply as *units*.) Programs consist of collections of units, which contain definitions of classes, objects, functions, and variables. At the simplest level, the addition of classes (and objects) suggests a new way to organize code.

One recent approach to object orientation, the Visual Basic 4.0 implementation, requires that you define each new class in a separate *class module*. See Chapter 7 for a detailed description of this OOP implementation.

Choose Your Language

In human languages, we often classify objects into hierarchies and extend our knowledge by relating the properties and behaviors we know (from base classes) to new subclasses. Using object-oriented programming techniques, you build programs in a similar manner: by creating new base classes (or types) and deriving more complex classes (or types) from them.

Three OOP terms in wide use—*user-defined types, abstract data types,* and *classes*—refer to a similar idea about programming. Don't let the language confuse you. OOP ideas aren't that complicated, and they're based on the way we organize our thoughts about objects.

Offer a child a new type of clothing, and she'll determine that it can be worn and probably try to put it on. Given a new type of container, you know that there must be a way to open and close it (even if it's child- or programmer-proof). Because you've driven bicycles, cars, boats, or airplanes, you know that vehicles share many characteristics while differing in others. For example, any vehicle can be steered. Although the steering mechanisms differ among vehicles, you can generalize about them. Then, faced with a new type of vehicle (for example, a spaceship), you can surmise that there's probably some way to steer it. We can say that `vehicle` is a base type and `spaceship` is a derived type.

Object-oriented programming languages mirror these ideas about the real world by letting you create *abstract data types* that act like built-in types. But they're special because you, or another programmer, have extended the language your compiler understands, creating a new type dynamically.

Abstract data types behave just like built-in types—they have internal data and external operations like a floating-point number, for example, that has an exponent, mantissa, and sign bit and knows how to add itself to another floating-point number.

User-defined types contain user-defined data (properties) and operations (behaviors). Although they look almost exactly like functions or procedures, user-defined operations are called *methods.* To call one of these methods, you "call" the object (in structured programming terms); in OOP, this is known as "sending a message to the object." For example, to stop a car object, you send it a *stop* message. Note that you tell the object what to do but not how to do it; the details of how to do it have been encapsulated.

About Inheritance and Composition

Once you've built a class, how do you extend its functionality? Do you barge in and change the code, perhaps introducing (*shudder!*) bugs? Not if you can help it. Once you've defined a new base type (or class), you can build on it using inheritance. When you create a new type from an existing type, the new type (sometimes called a *derived* type) automatically inherits all the properties and behaviors from the base type.

What do you put into a base class? Characteristics and behaviors that are shared by a class. For example, apples, oranges, and bananas are kinds of edible fruit. They have different specific characteristics, but each has a color and each can be eaten. Yet the methods you use to eat different kinds of fruit can differ. You have to peel a banana before you eat it, and you eat everything except the peel. You don't have to peel an apple, and you can eat the peel, but you don't eat the core.

At this point, you might be tempted to overrate (and subsequently overuse) inheritance when deciding how to design new classes of objects. Class hierarchies are wonderful tools, but not all information fits into tidy hierarchies. Sometimes it's better to focus on how you compose a class.

In some languages, such as C++, a class can *contain* other classes. For example, if `vehicle` is a base class and you derive a `car` class from `vehicle`, `car` inherits some basic properties and behaviors from the abstract `vehicle` class. But there's more to a car than that. A car consists of other objects (engine, wheels, and transmission, for example).

When deciding how to create classes and objects (instances of classes), you must always balance what should be derived (or inherited) with what should be encapsulated in methods and properties. A key question to ask yourself when testing inheritance: "Is my derived class inherently similar to its superclass?" If the answer is yes, use inheritance. Otherwise, focus on composition.

Another way of expressing OOP: You build family trees (or hierarchies) for data structures. Any type can have a long family tree, but, in general, each subclass has a single immediate ancestor. We call this *single* inheritance. Virtually all OOP implementations allow single inheritance. One, C++, allows classes to have more than one immediate ancestor; we call this *multiple* inheritance (see Figure 1.1). Delphi, dBASE for Windows, and Smalltalk allow single inheritance. Visual Basic, although allowing the encapsulation of data and procedures in a class (created in a class module), does not permit inheritance.

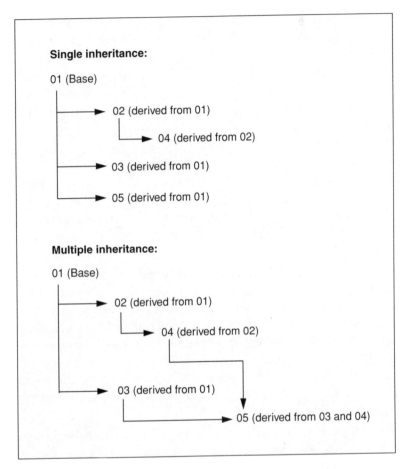

Figure 1.1 **Single and multiple inheritance.**

If inheritance sounds good, you might assume that multiple inheritance is even better. In fact, multiple inheritance has been hotly debated among language designers for years. In general, you can do anything in a single-inheritance language that you can in a multiple-inheritance language.

A difficulty arises with multiple inheritance when you combine several classes, each of which defines the same methods. Suppose that two classes—Sound and Graphic, are combined into a new class called Multimedia. Sound has the properties pitch, duration, and voice and the methods play, rescale, load, and store. Graphic has the properties bitmap, size, and color and the methods draw, rescale, load, and store. When you combine these into the new class, Multimedia, there's a conflict between the methods rescale, load, and store.

What does it mean for a Multimedia object to rescale itself? That depends on what you want to happen. Does it mean to rescale the sound at a different pitch (as with Sound) or fit in a smaller space (as with Graphic)? What if you attempt to load or store a Multimedia object? Should it store itself as a Sound or as a Graphic or write out both components? If it writes out both components, which order should be used? Should this order always be followed when there are conflicts? In most multiple-inheritance languages, you end up writing extra code to resolve the difficulty.

The problem is one of ambiguity. It may not be clear to the compiler in a multiple-inheritance language which operation should take precedence when conflicts arise. What's more, even if the compiler resolves the ambiguity, you as the programmer may have difficulty remembering the rules, particularly when debugging. Some language designers feel that multiple inheritance is essential. Most view it as a double-edged sword: It gives power and flexibility, but at the same time it can increase the complexity of programs. It has been called "the GoTo of the 1990s" because it adds convenience but can easily be misused.

When you want to implement in a single-inheritance language a new class that looks as if it needs multiple inheritance, rely on composition. This usually means inheriting from the most appropriate class and allowing a class to contain the object of the other type. If you combined Sound and Graphic, you would probably choose to define the Multimedia type to have two fields, each of which contained a Sound and a Graphic object. We would then need to define "pass-through" methods that specified unambiguously what would happen when a Multimedia object got a message such as rescale, load, or store.

Neither multiple inheritance nor single inheritance is perfect in all cases, and both can require a little bit of extra code to make up for differences in how they work. There will always be times when the tool you use takes you down the wrong path, but it's important to recognize the beauty of the path you take and use the tool as it's meant to be used. Perhaps a future path will go beyond the notion of multiple inheritance and take us to even better places.

Building a New Type

Let's say you've created a base type in C++:

```
class base {
public:
  int X,Y;
  void doSomethingWithXandY();
};
```

or in Delphi:

```
type
     Base = class(TObject)
        X,Y: integer;
         procedure doSomethingWithXandY;
     end;
```

Now you want to build a new type derived from the existing base type. You want the derived type to be identical to the base type, with one exception: You'll extend base by adding a method called doSomethingElse.

You build derived simply and quickly by inheriting from base. In C++:

```
class derived : public base {
public:
  void doSomethingElse();
};
```

In Delphi:

```
type
   Derived = class(Base)
     procedure doSomethingElse;
   end;
```

Because derived inherits all the properties and methods of base, you don't need to redefine them; you simply tell the compiler you want to derive a new type (derived) from a base type (base) and add the new method. Now you can doSomethingWithXandY and doSomethingElse to variables of type derived. In C++:

```
main() {
  derived d;
  d.x = 5;
  d.y = 8;
  d.doSomethingWithXandY();
  d.doSomethingElse();
}
```

In Delphi:

```
var
D: Derived;

With D do
  begin
    X:= 5;
    Y:= 8;
    doSomethingWithXandY;
    doSomethingElse;
  end;
```

Notice again that you don't have to pass X and Y to doSomethingElse; it inherited knowledge of them, along with everything else, from base.

Inheritance lets you build very complex data types without repeating a lot of code. The new type simply inherits a base level of characteristics and behavior from an ancestor. It can also reimplement, or overwrite, any method it chooses. This reimplementation of base-type methods in derived types is fundamental to the concept of polymorphism, which we'll get to in a moment.

Inheritance is useful for two reasons. The first reason is simple: If you're given a working object type (or class) that doesn't do exactly what you want, you can create a new object type from it with inheritance and add a few characteristics. Not only can you program quickly, but you can also isolate the existing code (which works) from your new, experimental code (which may not).

Inheritance among OOP Languages

Interestingly enough, object-oriented languages themselves exhibit inheritance as they build on concepts introduced in previous languages. Most traditional structured languages, including C, Pascal, and PL/I, have been heavily influenced by Algol. Simula, the first OOP language, also inherited characteristics of Algol but added the concepts of objects, classes, and messages. All OOP languages inherit some of the characteristics and behavior of programming in Simula, either directly or from its descendant, Smalltalk.

Although some of the inheritance is clearly from a single ancestor (for example, BCPL begat B, which begat C), many of the languages borrowed from two or more ancestors, demonstrating multiple inheritance. This is especially true of the hybrid languages, including Delphi and C++, which combine characteristics and behavior of object-oriented languages with those of their traditional base languages, Pascal and C. Note that this doesn't mean that Delphi has multiple inheritance. It doesn't; it's just built from the concepts of the languages that preceded it.

Overriding Behavior and Data

Inheritance lets us automatically use the data and methods of a base type. Even though you inherit methods, you can always override them to achieve different behavior. For example, you might create a descendant of a barchart type that draws in three dimensions. You like how most of the barchart type functions, but you want to handle your own implementation. You can. You're not locked into the implementation found in the base type.

What if you want to "subtract" behavior from a derived type? You can do that by reimplementing the method as a dummy method that does nothing at all. Note, however, that if you find yourself writing lots of dummy methods to subtract behavior, it may be a sign that the base type should be broken down further so that new derived subtypes can inherit less information.

In C++, reimplementing methods is easy. But overriding fields is a little more difficult and requires more careful planning. For example, you can't normally override the built-in types in structs without using variant types. One solution here is to make fields that must be overridden objects themselves. For example, if you have a car hierarchy and if different car models use different types of transmissions, then Transmission itself should be a class with derived types for Automatic, Manual, FiveSpeed, and so on. It may not always be obvious when to divide things into distinct classes, but it's good to experiment with classes that contain other classes.

About Polymorphism

Another important aspect of inheritance is *polymorphism*. Consider again your interaction with the world. When you learn to steer a bicycle, you learn something that can also be applied to a car or boat. When you pilot any of these vehicles, to steer it you don't have to think about which type of vehicle it is—you turn the controls in one direction, and the vehicle moves in that direction. If this is true in the world, why shouldn't it be true of programming?

Let's represent this system with a base object type (or class) called vehicle and derived object types called bicycle, car, and boat. Any vehicle can be steered, and vehicles do different things to steer themselves depending on their type. Vehicle can respond to a message called steer, so any type that inherits vehicle can also accept that message.

Thus, bicycles, cars, and boats can be steered because they're vehicles, although the method each specific type uses when it gets the steer message is different. Polymorphism. You tell the vehicle to steer itself (send it a steer message), and it figures out what to do with the message.

Why is this so important? *Reusability*. You don't have to reimplement everything each time you create a new type of vehicle; you build on the existing objects. An object-oriented program that steers vehicles doesn't have to be rewritten just because it needs to handle a new type of vehicle. It already knows that any vehicle can respond to the steer message and act accordingly.

Using polymorphism to create extensible programs is important because programmers can't know everything about a program or the problem it needs to solve while developing the program. Programs need to change in response to new information.

Word processors didn't know about desktop publishing when they were created; new features had to be added as user needs changed. The need to change and evolve has been a nemesis of software development because change is expensive, and the inability to change often leads to obsolescence.

Change must be considered an integral part of a program. New information might come from understanding a system in a new way or because the problem changes in the real world. Either way, change is inevitable. Polymorphism reflects that by letting you create extensible programs.

Behaviors such as steering a vehicle and opening a container can be common to a group of types but implemented differently for each (such as the mechanisms for steering a bicycle and steering a car). Using polymorphism, you can create a system that knows that vehicles can be steered but not how a particular vehicle will be steered; those details can come later. The system is extensible because you can add new types of vehicles (and new ways of steering) without redesigning the program.

Creating abstract data types and hierarchies of flexible, reusable objects is a powerful programming idea. People view the world in terms of types, so representing a real-world system as a program of base and derived types is a natural process. Ideally, the model of the system in the computer is a direct mapping of the system in the real world. This means that if the system in the real world changes, it's easy to change the model in the computer. This simplicity makes software design, development, and maintenance faster and cheaper.

The use of abstract and derived data types also helps localize the changes you make to a system. Using traditional function-oriented techniques, you may make a change that propagates bugs throughout the system. But changes in an object-oriented system tend to be localized in an object. Because the data and functions are in one package, changes aren't as likely to propagate bugs outside that package. Therefore, you can change part of a working system without disrupting the rest.

When people talk about objects, they often talk about the protocol they understand. We can think of protocol as the set of messages an object can respond to. Generally, you'll find that objects that share a common base type or are compatible with each other have the same protocol. When designing your objects, try to follow a consistent, generic protocol so that your objects are more easily reused.

Polymorphism lets you establish a common interface to a group of types (which are created by inheritance from the base type). This interface defines the messages an object can receive and what the protocol is.

If your system understands and uses the interface to the base without necessarily knowing the particulars of the derived types, you can more easily extend it. If you need to add a type to an existing system, you simply derive it from the base type. The system uses only the base interface, so it immediately knows what to do with your new type.

Delphi, for example, requires that every new class (or object type) be derived from a base class. Each `TObject` class in Delphi consists of methods that handle basic interactions with the Windows environment. Any new component you create in Delphi, for example, will be derived from the `TComponent` class. Even the simplest classes you create in Delphi will be based on an existing Delphi class.

You can easily create any number of variables of a type, even at run time. Libraries of abstract data types are easy to reuse in new applications and can be extended when used in conjunction with inheritance, even if you don't have the source code for the library.

For example, if you're creating a motel management system using someone else's general-purpose room type, you can create your own type, `motel_room`, by deriving from `room` and adding characteristics and behavior to tell the user whether the room is occupied, has been cleaned, needs painting, and so on. Thus, you can easily reuse code by using an existing type or by deriving from and adding to an existing type.

When you call (or invoke) a method for an object, you send a message to the object. A message is really a function or procedure call. Why is a distinction made between sending a message and calling a function or procedure? Normally, it's just like a function call: You knew when you wrote the code what would be executed for that call. But with polymorphism, the code to be executed isn't determined until run time. So sending a message makes a distinction—you send a message to an object of a generic type and let the object figure out which method to call. "Put on the item of clothing" will invoke different responses depending on whether the item is a hat or a shoe.

Throughout this book, I'll use *call*, *invoke*, and *send a message* more or less synonymously. After all, most of us have been calling and invoking functions for a long while.

Polymorphism means that a method can have one name that's shared throughout an object type hierarchy. Each object type may have a different implementation for the method. The name of the method is the same for each object type, but what it does is different.

Suppose you want to define `derived2`, which inherits the data and methods from `derived` and reimplements the method `doSomething Else`. You define it as follows in C++:

```
class derived2 : public derived {
public:
  void doSomethingElse();
};
```

and in Delphi:

```
type
   Derived2 = class (Derived)
       procedure doSomethingElse;
   end;
```

Now when you use a variable of type `derived2`, it will inherit the data fields from `derived` but can use its own `doSomethingElse` method.

When you send a message to an object, the compiler first looks to see whether the object's type (or class) definition contains the method you want. If it finds the method in the type definition, that's what it uses. If the type definition doesn't contain the method, the compiler searches the inheritance hierarchy until it finds the appropriate method. If it doesn't find the method in any ancestor, it reports an error.

Making the compiler search through the inheritance hierarchy for the correct method takes time and can decrease performance. The overhead is generally not great, especially in hybrid languages such as C++ and Delphi. However, there will be times when you want to reduce the impact by optimizing your code.

Although we think of inheritance as requiring a search up the hierarchy to find the correct method, this technique would have disastrous results for large applications; the more you used inheritance, the slower your program would get. No object-oriented language that I know of uses this kind of linear search. Instead, an efficient indirect function call is used so that only one additional instruction is required on a method call. In most cases, less code is required to do this "call indirect" than to mimic the flexibility of object-oriented programming using an `if`, `switch`, or `case` statement.

Static and Dynamic Binding

Each object created so far uses statically bound methods. Static binding (also called *early* binding) means that the compiler resolves all references to functions by the time the program is loaded. When you call a statically bound method, the compiler figures out exactly which function to call at compile time.

With polymorphism, you want to send a message to an object and let the object figure out which method to use. What you're asking the compiler to do is to resolve some references at run time. This is called *late*, or *dynamic*, binding.

Why is late binding important? Because it lets you defer decisions and connections until run time, thus making the system more flexible and easier to extend. It also means that you can give your objects general requests, and they can determine how to respond. You tell the objects what to do, and they figure out how to do it.

To resolve references to methods at run time, you create virtual methods. To create a virtual method in C++, add the keyword `virtual` to a function in the base class:

```
class aClass {
public:
  int X,Y;
  virtual void doSomethingWithXandY();
};
```

That's it; dynamic binding happens automatically for `doSomething WithXandY` in all classes derived from `aClass`. But there's a catch: A method can't be statically bound in one type and virtual in another. You must anticipate that by declaring these methods as virtual from the beginning. This is true in both C++ and Delphi, but in Delphi, the story is slightly different—you can use either the keyword `virtual` or `dynamic`, and `override` to indicate dynamic method binding.

In Delphi, the keywords `virtual` and `dynamic` allow you to redefine methods in descendent objects, but they differ in their dispatch mechanisms. The virtual directive creates an entry for the object in the object's virtual method table (or VMT). The VMT is an address container for all the virtual methods in a class (or object type). Instead of creating an entry in the VMT, the dynamic directive assigns unique reference numbers to each virtual method and stores these numbers in a table. You then use `over-ride` when you actually override a virtual method.

One other important difference between OOP languages is how they construct objects. In C++, a *constructor* is a special function that sets up the machinery for virtual methods and specifies how a new object type will be initialized. Uninitialized objects can be a major source of bugs—one important reason that C++ will handle construction for you automatically.

In Delphi, a constructor (method) called `Create` allocates memory for the new object (or instance of an object type) and points to the new object. You must invoke the `Create` method yourself. When you invoke it, you assign an instance (an object) to a variable. For example, create the following type:

```
type
        Employee = class (Tobject)
                Name: string[27];
                Title: string[22];
                Salary: Double;
                WeeksWorked: Integer;
                Vacation: Integer;
                function CalculateVacation: Integer;
        end;
```

Then use the `Create` method to declare an instance of `Employee` as follows:

```
var
        Employee1: Employee;
        Employee1 := Employee.Create;
```

In Delphi, you can also override the `Create` constructor and initialize variables during creation.

In C++ and Delphi, to cause late binding to occur, you use the `virtual` keyword when declaring a method in the base class. The method is then virtual in all its derived classes.

Virtual (or dynamic) methods allow derived types to have their own versions of a base type method. This is a powerful (but sometimes thorny) aspect of object-oriented programming, one we'll return to again and again as we explore *The Tao of Objects*.

Dynamic Programming

Object-oriented languages support a dynamic style of programming, allowing variables to be created and destroyed as easily at run time as at compile time. Think about it: The situations in which you know all the types and quantities of objects while you're writing the program are really the special cases. In general, you don't know those factors. In a CAD system, for example, you don't know until the program is running which shapes or types of shapes the user will want to display. Object-oriented programming is dynamic; it lets you design systems that are flexible enough to accommodate change.

C and Pascal programmers have been able to program dynamically for a long time. Dynamic memory allocation and pointers allow you to get and release space for variables at run time. You can decide when to create and destroy the variables and how many variables to use. You use a pointer to hold the address of a dynamically allocated chunk of memory. (You can think of a pointer as simply a way to change, at run time, the storage used by an identifier.)

Unfortunately, dynamically allocated memory in C and Pascal is a poor relation to a real variable. You have to treat dynamic memory as a special case, making it harder and less reliable to use. In C++ and Delphi, the ability to create and destroy real variables at run time was considered so important that it's now in the core of these languages in the form of constructors and destructors. When you create a new, user-defined object type, making a dynamic variable of that type is as easy as making an automatic variable.

This means you can easily build an object-oriented program that doesn't need to know the number or type of objects involved in a problem before it begins to solve it. This idea fits beautifully with the world, where you seldom know all the tools you'll need when you begin working on a project. Object-oriented languages allow you to write programs that adapt to new situations.

Another View

You might find it helpful to think of a program as an object. It has its own internal data and an interface through which you request operations and information. This is how you use, for example, a word processor (an object), which manages its own data. With the keyboard, you send the word processor such messages as "insert this character" and "delete that word."

Writing an object-oriented program is also like using a computer that allows you to run more than one program at once. You might use a communication program to fetch data, a spreadsheet to analyze it, and a word processor to prepare a report. Although you can (in theory, at least) write any of these programs yourself, you don't have to. It's easier to use programs someone else has written.

When you request data (a report, for example), you only want to see the report. Building a program using objects is similar. You "run" objects (just as you run programs) that perform various tasks. You may write the code for these objects or use someone else's. The program consists of objects and the messages you send them.

By now, you should be getting the message that a program is a static implementation of a solution. Object-oriented programming is a process for anticipating change in programs, one that lets them adapt to new situations.

Classes, User-Defined Types, and Object Types: Three Names, One Idea

Although structured languages such as Pascal, C, and Modula-2 allow you to combine data and functions in distinct packages called *units, files,* or *modules,* these languages don't let you manipulate these packages of code as if they were built-in types.

Built-in types are special because the compiler knows how to handle them before you ever write a line of code. In contrast, the compiler must learn how to handle types that aren't built-in.

Units, files, and modules do help organize and coordinate code, but they don't explicitly establish or maintain relationships among their components. Neither the data nor the functions in a module, unit, or file are explicitly protected. Thus, unless you declare data locally (within functions), any function in any module can manipulate and possibly corrupt the data. If you declare a data element locally, you make it safer but limit access to a single function. If you declare it globally, everyone can get at it—definitely a dilemma.

Object-oriented languages give you a way out by introducing a new kind of structure that protects data elements and creates specific relationships for them. This new structure, as you've learned already, is a class, or user-defined object type, or just plain object type, depending on the OOP language. The compiler knows about object types and treats them as if they were built into the language. But, although object types are key to object-oriented programming, not all object-oriented languages treat them exactly the same way.

In general though, you'll find the following keywords—`private`, `public`, and `protected`—are used to control access in robust OOP languages.

❏ *Public* means that anyone can use it. Any methods following the keyword can be accessed only by methods declared within the same class.

❏ *Private* means that any members following the keyword can be accessed only by member functions declared within the same class.

❏ *Protected* means that any members following the keyword can be accessed by member functions within the same class and by member functions of classes derived from this class. For example, in C++:

```
class Access   {
   int X;        // private by default
   int Y;        // private by default

public:
   Access();     // Constructor is public and can be accessed
                 // from anywhere within the same scope.

private:
   int X;        // explicitly declared private

protected:
   int A;        // can now be accessed by any class
};               // derived from Access
```

Also, in C++, `Friends` are functions that are given permission to access a class's private data. You declare `friend` functions within a class declaration, as follows:

```
class Has_friends {
    int X;                  // X and Y are private by default.
  int Y;
public:
  Has_friends();
  ~Has_Friends();
  friend void Access_X_Y();
};
```

The function `Access_X_Y()` isn't one of the methods of `Has_ friends'`, but it can access the private characteristics, X and Y, because it's a friend.

An object type protects data by establishing the relationships between data and methods. Data can be accessed only by methods explicitly created for accessing the data or by functions outside the type given permission to access the data. You're less likely to manipulate the wrong data with the right methods and vice versa.

When you plan and define object types thoroughly enough, users of the object won't want or need to access its characteristics directly; they'll access them by sending a message to the object, which will in turn access its own data.

Once you define an object type (or class), anyone can use it without knowing specifically how it's implemented. Object types are a fundamental difference between object-oriented languages and traditional procedural languages.

About Types

The concept of *type* is essential to programming. The type of a variable tells us the range of values or states it can assume and the operators you can apply to it. Specific instances of a type have values or states determined by the operators that can manipulate them.

For example, in C++, any variable of type `int` can have a value from –32,768 to 32,767 and can be added, subtracted, multiplied, divided, compared, and so on. An integer in Delphi has the same range. A `longint` (in Delphi) or a `long` (in C++) can have a value in the range –2,147,483,648 to 2,147,483,647 and can be added, multiplied, and so on.

Types come in all shapes and sizes (one byte, two bytes, four bytes, eight bytes, and so on) and are either built into the language or built from simpler types.

The built-in types in C++ are `char`, `int`, `float`, and `double`. Four specifiers—`long`, `short`, `signed`, and `unsigned`—expand these simple types into a larger set. A structured type (such as `array` or `struct`) holds more than one simple type. These and others, such as pointers, are built into the language. The compiler already knows how to handle these types and doesn't have to learn about them each time it encounters an instance of one.

Pascal has a slightly different group of built-in types that the compiler knows about in advance (`Integer`, `Char`, `String`, `Real`, `Pointer`, `PChar` and `Boolean`). The integer and real types are further expanded to include short int `Long  int`, `Byte`, `Word`, `Single`, `Double`, `Extended`, and `Comp`. The compiler, too, can handle these types without having to learn about them.

To define an instance of a built-in type, you simply name a variable and specify its type. (When you define a variable, you create space for it; when you declare a variable, you tell the compiler that space exists for it and what it looks like.)

You define an instance of a built-in type in C++ as follows:

```
int AnyNumber;
```

In Delphi:

```
AnyNumber : integer;
```

Declaring a composite type of built-in types is almost as simple. In C++:

```
struct Numbers {
  int X;
  double Y;
};
```

and in Delphi:

```
Numbers = record
  X : Integer;
  Y: Double;
end;
```

A type describes the general characteristics and behaviors of a group of related objects. A variable is an instance of the type. OOP languages, such as C++, Delphi, and dBASE for Windows, make it easy to package, extend, and use these user-defined types. This new ability encourages you to rethink how you create systems and write code.

To create your own object types, you declare the type, and then define an instance of it. In C++, you can declare a class to represent the characteristics and behaviors of fruit:

```
// Enumerated types — colors and sizes;
// these can also be declared inside the class.
enum Colors {red, yellow, green, brown, orange};
enum Sizes {small, medium, large};

class AnyFruit {
  colors Color;      // private by default
  sizes Size;
public:
  void Growth_behavior();
};
```

In Delphi:

```
Colors = (red, yellow, green, brown, orange);
Sizes = (small, medium, large);

AnyFruit = class (TObject)
   private
       Color : colors;
       Size : sizes;
   public
```

```
        procedure Growth_behavior;
end;
```

You can then define a variable of the type in C++, as follows:

```
aFruit AnyFruit;
```

where the variable aFruit is an instance of the class AnyFruit. In Delphi, the declaration is:

```
AnyFruit : aFruit;
```

You implement classes by implementing their methods, just as you implement functions in C++ and procedures and functions in Delphi.

A possible implementation of the Growth_behavior method in C++ is:

```
void AnyFruit :: Growth_behavior()
{
  if (size != large)        // Check enumerated values.
    size++;
};
```

and in Delphi:

```
procedure AnyFruit.Growth_behavior;
begin
  If (Size <> large) then
    Size := Size + 1;
end;
```

The compiler treats user-defined object types just like types built into the language. Growth_behavior already knows about Size (they're part of the same type, AnyFruit), so you don't have to pass Size to it.

Constructors and Destructors

When you define an instance of a built-in type, the compiler creates space for it in memory. In effect, the compiler constructs the variable. When the variable is no longer needed, the compiler releases the space it used. In other words, it destroys the variable.

To make user-defined types as similar as possible to built-in types, the compiler needs comparable construction and destruction power. With built-in types, the compiler already knows the size of each type. When you define an object type, the compiler must figure out how much space to allocate and deallocate for it.

In C++, if you don't supply a constructor (or constructors—there can be more than one) and a destructor (there can only be one) for a class, the compiler automatically constructs and destroys the class the simplest way it can. If the simplest way isn't sufficient, you can define your own.

The constructor in C++ is a method with the same name as the class. The class destructor is the class name preceded by a tilde (~). The following fragment declares a class, AnyClass, with a constructor and destructor:

```
class AnyClass {
public:
  AnyClass;          // constructor
  ~AnyClass;         // destructor
};
```

In Delphi, construction and destruction occur through the Create and Free methods:

```
type
   AnyObject = object (TObject)
var
   ObjectInstance: AnyObject
   AnyObject.Create;{ construct object }
   AnyObject.Free;  { destroy object }
```

You can also have the constructor do something during initialization with an object's characteristics. The declaration in C++ is:

```
class Gauge {
  int Temp;              // private characteristics by default
  int Pressure;
public:
```

```
  Gauge(int Init_Temp, int Init_Pressure);      // constructor
  ~Gauge();
};
```

Here's the implementation:

```
Gauge::Gauge(int Init_Temp, int Init_Pressure);
  Temp = Init_temp;
  Press = Init_pressure;
};
```

The declaration in Delphi is:

```
Gauge = object
  Temp : integer;    { public by default }
  Pressure : integer;
  procedure Create (Init_Temp : integer; Init_Pressure : inte-
ger); virtual;
end;
```

and the implementation:

```
procedure Gauge.Create(Init_Temp : integer;
                       Init_pressure : integer);
begin
  Temp := Init_temp;
  Pressure := Init_pressure;
end;
```

Messages

Conventional programming systems typically view a program as a collection of procedures. Procedures are the active components; data are passive. If you declare data globally, any procedure can get at them, and the likelihood of incorrect data manipulation is high.

If you declare data locally (within a procedure), only that procedure can access it; the data are safer, but this is an overly restricted practice. What's needed is more flexibility so that data can be accessed by any number of defined procedures. In object-oriented programming, a method knows which data it can manipulate, and data know which methods can manipulate them.

In a procedural program, the flow of control is determined by the ordering of procedures and control mechanisms, such as `if`, `while`, `switch`, and so on. This implies that we know how to structure the entire program during program creation. In programs designed to capture the essence of a dynamic world, this assumption is unrealistic. The world is changing, and our ideas and models of the world must adapt. A better alternative captures the design flow in terms of logical relationships among objects.

Object-oriented programming captures these logical relationships in objects, and the flow of control in an object-oriented program is determined by the messages sent to objects. When you send a message, you clarify the communication among the components of a program. Objects respond to the messages sent to them and can send messages to other objects.

The term *message* is somewhat unfortunate because it's easily confused with *method* and seems to imply that operations take place asynchronously (like broadcast messages on a network or phone messages in an office). In fact, messages are implemented as indirect function calls and thus take place immediately, just like a traditional function call.

Messages, rather than data, move around the system. Instead of saying, "Invoke a function on a piece of data" (the procedural approach), you say, "Send a message to an object" (the object-oriented approach). To send a message to an object, you specify the object and the method you want to invoke.

Let's say you've declared the following `Point` type in C++:

```
class Point {
    int X;
    int Y;
public:
    int state;
    Point(int InitX, int InitY);    // constructor
    int IsVisible();                // Is point on or off?
};                                  // Return state.
```

The characteristics of Point are its location on the screen (*x*- and *y*- coordinates). Its behaviors are to construct itself and to say whether it's visible.

You can define an instance of Point and initialize it at the same time using Point's constructor:

```
int Visible;
Visible = Point ThisPoint(5,10); // Define/initialize ThisPoint.
```

You can then ask ThisPoint whether it's visible by sending it a message:

```
ThisPoint.IsVisible();
```

You can define a similar Point type in Delphi:

```
Point = class (TObject)
  X : integer;
  Y : integer;
  State : integer;
  procedure Create(InitX, InitY : integer); virtual;
  function IsVisible: integer;    { Is the point on or off? }
                            { Return state. }
end;
```

In Delphi, you use two lines of code to first declare the Point object and then initialize it by calling the constructor:

```
var

ThisPoint : Point;

begin
  ThisPoint.Create(5,10);
end;
```

You can ask ThisPoint whether it's visible by sending it a message:

```
var
  Visible : integer;
```

```
begin
  Visible := ThisPoint.IsVisible;
end;
```

Sending a message means calling an object's method, which manipulates or interprets the type's characteristics. In other words, if you want something done, you send a message to an instance of an object type, and the object handles it. Sending messages is a crucial aspect of object-oriented programming.

Stepping Back and Forward

This chapter has introduced classes, objects, and object-oriented programming techniques, focusing on the three cornerstones of OOP: encapsulation, inheritance, and polymorphism. These are the principal building blocks you'll use in the following chapters as you learn more about objects and how to design applications with OOP techniques.

You might say that little has changed in the fundamentals of OOP since the first edition of *The Tao of Objects* in 1990. For example, C++ still implements OOP its way and still remains the standard hybrid language implementation.

But much has changed because higher-level development applications such as Delphi, Visual Basic, and dBASE for Windows have chosen to build aspects of object orientation into their environments. The object-oriented nature of these (and other) applications makes this version of *The Tao of Objects* relate a different story. OOP has arrived, and is arriving.

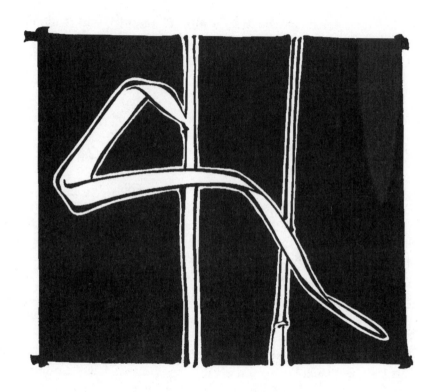

Chapter Two

Thinking in Objects

The world is formed from the void, like utensils from a block of wood. The master knows the utensils, yet keeps to the block: thus he can use all things.

In the practice of the Tao, every day something is dropped.

—Lao-tzu

The ability to create user-defined types (or classes) helps clarify relationships between data and operations, between distinct blocks of code, and between the world and our programming model of the world.

Classes are more powerful than units (or modules) because you can create and destroy instances of classes at runtime. This is a powerful idea, and one recent OOP implementation, Visual Basic 4.0, combines aspects of modules and classes to create a new entity: a class module. An instance of a class created within a class module can be created and destroyed by users at run time.

Real-world events are dynamic, and systems that model or simulate real-world events require that user-defined types be able to be created and destroyed on the fly. At run time.

Whereas most programming languages treat programs (and the modules or units that compose them) as static entities, object-oriented languages let programs anticipate change, both in themselves and in the world they model. A user-defined type can do anything a module can (and considerably more).

A big problem, even if you agree that objects are useful, is envisioning them. What should go into an object? What should its boundaries be? Should the object be big or small? More or less general? And how restrictive? Should it include a built-in capacity for change?

You create programs to answer questions about the world outside the program. A program represents your interaction with that world. The program is a tool to help you model or understand that world. Because that world consists of objects, object-oriented programs are a natural way to organize your representations of the world's objects. OOP helps you (or attempts to help you) reduce the time it takes to translate the objects of the world into a program.

For fun (one of the best reasons I can think of to program) and to loosen up your object-oriented thinking, let's examine a few of the many objects in the real and computing worlds. We'll just describe (or prototype) things without worrying about implementation details.

One design implication of OOP is that you can sketch a system, develop its interface, and delay writing the implementation code. You can see whether things work at the earliest possible moment (for example, when your code compiles) without linking in all the modules that use the interface. This saves time and encourages you to experiment rather than become locked into ideas. And if you plan your interface well, you can isolate the code you need to change and can isolate errors in code.

How can you represent a simple object such as a clock? Let's say it consists of the characteristics current_hour, current_minute, alarm_hour, and alarm_minute and the behaviors tick (the mechanism for running the clock), set_alarm, and get_alarm_status. You could describe it like this in C++:

```
class clock {
  int current_hour;
  int current_minute;
  int alarm_hour;
  int alarm_minute;
public:
  clock();            // Initialize current hour and minute.
  int get_alarm_status(); // Return 1 if alarm is on.
  int set_alarm();        // Return 1 if alarm is set.
  void tick();
};
```

or like this in Delphi:

```
Clock = class (TObject)
  private
      Current_hour: integer;
      Current_minute : integer;
      Alarm_hour : integer;
      Alarm_minute: integer;
  public
      function get_alarm_status: integer;
      function set_alarm: integer;
      procedure tick;
end;
```

Or how about an object type to describe the clothing worn by a fashion model? In C++:

```
char underwear[12];
char shirt[15];
char socks[8];
```

```
enum Clothes (underwear, shirt, socks);

class Fashion_Model{
    his_underwear underwear;        // private by default
public:
      his_shirt shirt;              // public by declaration
protected:
      his_socks socks;              // protected by declaration
};
```

In Delphi:

```
var

Underwear : string[12];
Shirt : string [15];
Socks : string [8];

type

Clothes = (Underwear, Shirt, Socks);

Fashion_Model = class(TObject)
    public                      { public to unit by declaration }
        Shirt : His_shirt;
        Socks : His_socks;
    private
        Underwear : His_underwear; { private to unit }
end;
```

How about a window? Not the one you're looking out of now, but one on your gloriously colored VGA screen. Let's define one consisting of dimensions, a title box, a border state, and a way to change the border state. In C++:

```
class Window {
  int X1;              // upper left
```

```
    int Y1;        // upper left
    int X2;        // bottom right
    int Y2;        // bottom right
    char Title[40];
    int border_state;
public:
    void change_border_state();
};
```

In Delphi:

```
Window = class(TObject)
private
    X1 : integer; (* upper left *)
    Y1 : integer; (* upper left *)
    X2 : integer; (* upper right *)
    Y2 : integer; (* upper right *)
    Title : string[40];
    Border_state : integer;
public
    procedure Change_border_state;
end;
```

Don't fret that the window is too simple. Part of the beauty of object-oriented programming is that it lets you extend objects without penalty. If you want to create a fancier window, derive it from this one.

The first way you should think about objects is in small, simple chunks. The second way is to think generally by imagining the fundamental concepts, properties, and behaviors of objects.

Consider a buffer, in this case a structure for holding chars or strings. Give it the characteristics size, front, and rear and a constructor to initialize the buffer. In C++:

```
class Buffer {
    char buf[255];
    int size;
    int front;
```

```
    int rear;
public:
  Buffer()          // constructor to init Buffer
  ~Buffer();        // destructor
};
```

The constructor initializes the buffer by setting each char to 0. In C++:

```
Buffer::Buffer() {
    int count;
    for (count = 0; count < 256; buf[count] = 0; count++);
};
```

In Delphi:

```
  Buffer = class (TObject)
  Buf     :   string[255];
  Size    :   integer;
  Front   :   integer;
  Rear    :   integer;
  constructor Create;
end;
```

The constructor implementation is:

```
constructor Buffer.Create;
var
  Count : integer;
begin
  For Count := 1 to 255 do
    Buf[Count] := '0';
end;
```

This simple buffer might not be what you had in mind. You might want to add and delete items from the buffer, for example. Don't fret; you can add the parts you need as you go along. When you first imagine an object, think of it only as an experiment, a beginning. Object-oriented programming encourages this peaceful kind of thinking.

Imagine that you need to simulate the activity of a group of teachers to develop an efficient schedule for a school. You can think of teachers as objects and describe them in terms of the behavior that affects the school's schedule. You might need to know what their free periods are, which subjects they can teach, how they teach, and so on. You could represent a teacher as follows in C++:

```
enum Subjects {music, English, physics, biology, calculus}

class Teacher {
  int FreePeriod;
  subjects Subject;
public:
  Teacher();              // Construct a teacher.
  ~Teacher();             // Destroy a teacher.
  void Teaching_Behavior();
};
```

In Delphi:

```
Subjects = (music, English, physics, biology, calculus);

Teacher = object
  FreePeriod: Integer;
  Subject : subjects;
  procedure Teaching_behavior();
end;
```

You might then build a complete scheduling system from a group of objects: teacher, students, school, and so forth. There might be different types of teachers, each inheriting from the abstract type shown above.

Complex Numbers

A complex number represents a point on a plane. You can represent this point using either Cartesian (an x,y pair) or polar coordinates (an angle from an axis and a distance), as shown in Figures 2.1 and 2.2. A type for manipulating complex numbers might consist of methods for returning the values of x and y (the Cartesian representation), returning the distance and an angle (the polar representation), adding complex numbers, and so on.

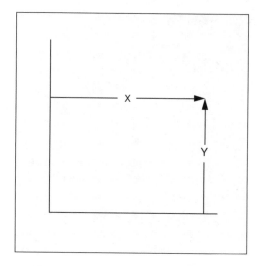

Figure 2.1 **Cartesian coordinates.**

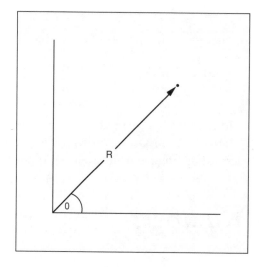

Figure 2.2 **Polar coordinates.**

Here's one possible declaration in C++:

```
class Complex {
  float X, Y, Distance, Angle;
public:
  float FindX();            // Return X.
  float FindY();            // Return Y.
  float FindDistance();     // Return Distance.
  float FindAngle();        // Return Angle.
  float Add();              // Return sum.
};
```

In Delphi:

```
Complex = class (TObject)
  public
      X, Y, Distance, Angle : real;
      function FindX : real;
      function FindY : real;
      function FindDistance : real;
      function FindAngle : real;
      function Add: real;          { Return sum. }
end;
```

Operator Overloading in C++

You can easily define methods such as add, subtract, and so on for a complex number class in C++ or Delphi. However, using add or subtract in place of + or − isn't quite consistent with the built-in types for integers or floating-point numbers. In C++, you can use operator overloading to define methods that are the same as any of the built-in operators.

Strictly speaking, operator overloading isn't a requirement in object-oriented programming; rather, it's another example of "syntactic sugar" because it makes things look more like what the programmer has in mind. It's a nice touch, though, particularly in mathematical and scientific programming.

Types, Not Individuals

It's important to realize that you're interested less in individual objects than in abstract types of objects. When you create a type, you need to imagine not the specific case, but the general case. If you're modeling a system that needs to describe employees, create a type that represents the general class of employees and go from there, creating instances and deriving subtypes.

In C++:

```
class employee {
  char last_name [28];
  char first_name [15];
  double employee_id;
  double SS_number;
  float salary;
  void do_job();
};
```

In Delphi:

```
Employee = class(TObject)
  Last_name : string[28];
  First_name : string[15];
  Employee_id : double;
  SS_number : double;
  Salary : real;
  procedure do_job;
end;
```

An individual of the `employee` type is an instance of `employee`. In C++:

```
employee AnEmployee;
```

In Delphi:

```
AnEmployee : Employee;
```

Here are a few things to keep in mind when you're creating classes (or object types):

- ❑ Classes may (or likely will) need to be extended.
- ❑ Methods within the class may be customized, overridden, or reimplemented by descendants.
- ❑ The classes exist within a system, which will also need to be extended, most likely into a hierarchy of classes.

How Complex Should Objects Be?

When you define objects, try to balance functionality and reusability. Resist the urge to create large "kitchen sink" object types that do everything. Big objects are hard to understand and, worse, hard to reuse. Instead, try to create object types that have a single, well-defined purpose. This will make it easier to reuse objects in various applications. For example, a word processor might consist of many objects, such as a text buffer, a formatter, a printer, a window, a menu, and so on. Some of these objects—windows and menus, for example—might be reused in a spreadsheet.

Simpler classes are easier to understand and maintain. If you start creating classes that can't be explained in a few sentences or have more than 50 or 60 methods, it's time to break the classes down into smaller pieces.

Base and Abstract Types

A base type defines a *common interface* to a group of similar types. A base type generalizes the intended uses for a hierarchy of types. In other words, it describes the range of messages, or protocol, that an object of a type can respond to.

Object-oriented programming clearly distinguishes the interface from the implementation. Type declarations go in the interface. The interface says, "Here's what a type looks like, and here are its behaviors." It doesn't specify how the type behaves; it leaves that to the implementation.

The interface must be visible everywhere a type is used. The implementation must be in only one spot. From a design perspective, this allows you to prototype code (via the interface) without implementing it. This should reduce errors; you can modify the implementation without disturbing the interface.

A base type can be simple. In C++:

```
class Base {
public:
  Base();
  ~Base();
};
```

In Delphi:

```
Base = class (TObject)
end;
```

> **Note:** All Delphi classes are derived from an existing base class. Even the simplest base class you create in Delphi must be derived from a "system" class. In contrast, both C++ and dBASE for Windows allow class declarations that are not based on any exisiting class.

A base type can also be more complex. In C++:

```
class Base {
  int Some_characteristic;
public:
  Base();
  ~Base();
  void Behavior1();
  void Behavior2();
  void Behavior3();          // and so on
};
```

In Delphi:

```
Base = class (TObject)
  Some_characteristic : integer;
  procedure Behavior1;
  procedure Behavior2;
  procedure Behavior3;
end;
```

A class (or object type) is a useful concept. Some OOP implementations, such as Visual Basic 4.0, consider it enough. Although object-based in most respects and object-oriented in allowing programmers to create new classes, Visual Basic does not provide a mechanism for creating hierarchies. But knowledge about the world is often visualized more clearly through hierarchies: An aspen is a type of deciduous tree, a type of woody plant, and a type of living entity. In most OOP implementations, a mechanism for creating hierarchies is integral. A base type is a node in the hierarchy and can itself be a derived type.

Base can be the head of a hierarchy:

```
01 (base)
  |————————→02 (derived from 01)
  |       └————→04 (derived from 02)
  |————————→03 (derived from 01)
  └————————→05 (derived from 01)
```

a node in a hierarchy:

```
04 ( another base)
  |————————→06 (derived from 04)
  |————————→07 (a new base, derived from 04)
  |————————→08 (derived from 04)
  └————————→09 (derived from 04)
```

and subsequently a Base for another hierarchy:

```
07 ( another base)
  |————————→10 (derived from 07)
  |————————→11 (derived from 07)
  └————————→12 (derived from 07)
```

When we use a base type strictly for creating other object types, we typically call it an *abstract* type. An abstract type has no instances. It simply specifies an interface for all types derived from it. Or in slightly different terms, an abstract class "abstracts" the behaviors and properties that are common among a hierarchical group of classes. You might think of abstract types as pathways for creating and extending any hierarchical object-oriented system.

C++ explicitly supports abstract classes via the pure *virtual* function. This keyword tells the compiler to resolve references to a method at run time. When you call a statically bound method—the typical pre–object-oriented way—the compiler figures out at compile time exactly which function to call. Static (or early) binding means that the compiler allocates and resolves all references to functions at compile time. In an object-oriented system, you want to send a message to an object and let the object decide how to respond.

You're asking the compiler to resolve some references at run time (late or dynamic binding). To resolve references to methods at run time, you create virtual methods. These allow derived types to have their own versions of a base-type method.

In C++, you specify that a virtual function is pure by assigning its definition to zero:

```
class abstract {
//...
public:
  abstract()
  virtual void behavior() = 0;
//...
};
```

Delphi also allows explicit assignment during the interface using the keyword Abstract. Or you can alternately declare an abstract object in Delphi, describe its interface and make its definition empty:

```
Abstract = class (TObject)
 procedure Behavior; virtual;
end;
```

Its implementation is:

```
procedure Abstract.Behavior;
begin
end;
```

In C++, you can alternatively use the standard procedure, `Abstract`, when implementing an abstract object type. This will ensure that attempts to use instances of the abstract type will cause a run-time error.

An abstract class supports the idea of generality. The classic example of an abstract class is a shape, which might consist of concrete variants such as ellipse, circle, cylinder, cone, rectangle, triangle, and pentagon. By definition, an abstract class in C++ can be used only as a base class of another class.

If you use abstract object types, you can change the interface and immediately propagate changes throughout the system. All changes to the abstract type are retroactive through its derived types.

Abstract vs. Concrete

No formal language distinction exists between how you declare abstract data types and how you declare "concrete" or derived classes. But you do find differences at the implementation level in how classes are defined and used. Abstract types, by their nature, usually aren't complete; they tend to have some abstract methods that are implemented only in descendant types. Abstract types are important tools for developing a system of reusable objects.

In general, try to design general-purpose classes; then derive subclasses that solve specific problems. This will improve reusablity. You can create layers of classes that build upon each other, each becoming a bit more concrete, a bit more problem-specific, as you move down the hierarchy.

Public and Private

This chapter's object examples have used the keywords `private` and `public` often. As far as I know, there are no etched-in-stone rules about when you should use these and other keywords. One question you might ask is, "Where should a property or method be visible?"

For example, in Delphi, during component creation, you use modules and units when developing classes. In this case, you should put related classes in the same module or unit so that they can access each other's private properties and methods without making those private parts known to other modules. Inside a module, private identifiers act as if they were public. Outside the module, private identifiers are unknown and thus inaccessible. The scope of "private" identifiers is the module containing the class declaration.

Typically, you want a user (and perhaps objects) to be able to modify the properties of visual objects or components (such as text boxes and buttons). If so, make the properties for components public. Public declarations can be accessed outside the current module.

Planning for Change

A system developed using object-oriented techniques allows you to reuse and extend others' code without having access to source code. The only requirement is that the designers and coders of the classes you want to reuse planned for change by creating abstract classes, creating classes that are general enough to allow themselves to be extended, and using virtual methods.

When defining your own object types, you should consider how your types relate to the types they model in the real world and how reusable they are. For example, the following code segment creates an abstract user-defined type (called AnyClass in C++ and AnyObject in Delphi) that contains a virtual abstract AnyBehavior method. This method allows any class or object derived from AnyClass or AnyObject to create its own AnyBehavior method.

In C++ :

```
class AnyClass {
public:
  AnyClass;                         // constructor
  ~AnyClass;                        // destructor
  virtual void AnyBehavior() = 0;
};
```

In Delphi:

```
AnyObject = class (TObject)
  procedure AnyBehavior; virtual;
end;
```

You don't know how any future types derived from AnyClass or AnyObject will implement AnyBehavior. AnyClass and AnyObject are generalizations and thus can easily be extended to create any number of specific types and behaviors. Classes and objects built this way (from abstract, extensible types) can be distributed in libraries that can themselves be extended, even without access to the library's source code, through inheritance. To extend the library, you simply derive a new object type and reimplement its virtual behaviors.

The Trickle-Up Theory

You'll find that your first attempts at creating reusable abstract types aren't very successful. A method here or there is missing, and you end up implementing something in the derived object type. If you create another derived type, you may find yourself writing almost the same code. With careful attention to these situations, you'll be able to make these two methods more general-purpose and move them up to the base type.

This is what I call the "trickle-up theory." It says that as you implement new descendant types, you often find some of the functionality moving up into the base type, where it can also be inherited by other derived types. This happens to even the most experienced object-oriented programmers and is part of the dynamic evolution of object types.

Until you've successfully reused base objects two or three times with new derived types, you'll find that some changes are required. But if you keep at it, you'll become better at solving general problems and will eventually create abstract types almost instinctively.

Objects, Classes, and Types

Objects are all around us. They help us learn, remember, and organize our lives. We group the world (often subconsciously) into related object types.

For example, dogs represent a template for a group of dogs with similar characteristics and behaviors. `Malamute`, `Labrador Retriever`, and `German Shepherd` are subtypes of the type `Dog`. My dog Luke is an instance of the subclass `Labrador Retriever` of class `Dog`.

`Font` is a name we use to depict the size and shape of characters. It's a type (no pun intended) that can consist of many subtypes, such as `Courier`, `Prestige`, `Tiffany`, and so on. The list of types (classes or objects) goes on and on.

This book is a plan for anticipating growth and change in the world in which you live and work. A common pitfall of procedural systems is what is sometimes called "the one-function solution": You assume that you're writing code as if there's only one instance of a problem. The solution is hard-wired into the system. When faced with a slightly different problem later, you have to redesign the system. Not a good approach.

When you create a new class (or object type), you're extending the abilities of the language. And by establishing an interface to a group of types, you open the door for the sensible development of huge projects. This interface can remain the same even if you later improve the implementation, so you can modify code without affecting the rest of the system.

The interface of a type is enforced by the compiler, not by a person or a set of guidelines. This makes the integration of types into the final product much easier and simpler. The compiler enforces the proper use of the type, ensures the proper initialization and cleanup of objects, and verifies that message passing is performed properly.

Object-oriented programming offers the best organizational techniques I know of for anticipating and incorporating change in program development.

It's as easy to create a type as it is to create an individual—almost. And once you've created a type, you can generate an entire system of types from it through inheritance.

Although many of the benefits of encapsulation are convenient for small programming projects, encapsulation is particularly valuable when you begin to "program in the large." It helps you build programs more quickly and easily.

Many languages can easily handle small to medium-sized programs; the problems crop up when the programs get really big. C and Pascal (and their descendants C++ and Delphi), with extensions for separate compilation, allow programming in the large, but little nuisances of the languages become tremendous liabilities when you're creating large programs. They can easily bring a project to its knees.

The little inconveniences become important as the system grows. C++ and Delphi, by supporting encapsulation and the rules associated with the new data types, remove many of the problems that prevent programming in the large. This means not only that a big team working on a big project can easily construct and integrate the system but also that a small team or a single person, using predefined types created for earlier projects or distributed by vendors, can build and maintain systems they previously couldn't have conceived of. This opens up amazing possibilities for creativity.

Chapter Three

Extending the System

To find the origin, trace back the manifestations. When you recognize the children, and find the mother, you'll be free of sorrow.

—Lao-tzu

Like modern physicists, Buddhists see all objects as processes in a universal flux, and deny the existence of any material substance.

—Fritjof Capra

We learn about, use, and organize objects in the world by classifying them into general and specific types based on their similarities and differences in properties and behaviors. For example, mandolins, fiddles, banjos, and guitars are all types of stringed musical instruments. They share the behaviors that they can be played and that playing them makes music. They have a common property (or state) of being in or out of tune.

The way you play each instrument depends on its characteristics. One characteristic is the number of strings. A mandolin has eight strings, a fiddle four, a banjo four or five, and a guitar four, six, (rarely eight), or twelve. Mandolin, fiddle, banjo, and guitar are specific types of the general type stringed musical instrument. Using object-oriented programming, you can express this kind of specification with inheritance.

Through inheritance, an object type inherits all the characteristics of an existing type and adds specific characteristics or behaviors of its own. Examples of inheritance are common. In the programming world, for example, you can organize languages by classifying them into a base type and specific types derived from it. Figure 3.1 shows how you might do that. Beginning with a general type (language), you could derive the specific types (functional, imperative, and logical) and the more specific types (C, Pascal, LISP, Prolog, C++, Delphi, and Prolog++).

In this scenario, C and Pascal are derived from imperative and thus have features in common with all imperative languages. C++ is derived, in turn, from C. And Delphi is derived from Pascal. C++ and Delphi are extended: imperative languages with object-oriented extensions.

The simplest way to extend a system is to add new features to an existing type. In the language hierarchy, Prolog is a type of logic language. Prolog++ is a type of Prolog, extended by the addition of object-oriented features. Extension in this case is mostly organizational.

In a more complex scenario, you extend a system by adding subtypes to it without disrupting outside control of the system.

Imagine a system consisting of functions for controlling related shapes (Figure 3.2). Using object-oriented techniques, you can add a new shape to the system without changing the shape controller (Figure 3.3).

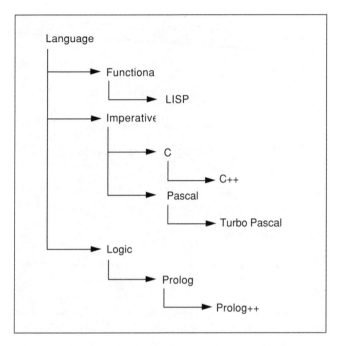

Figure 3.1 **Beginning with a general type** (Language),
you can derive specific types.

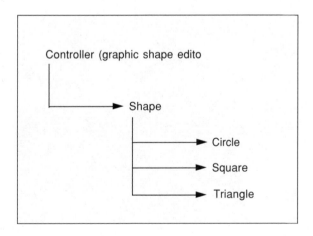

Figure 3.2 **A system consisting of functions for controlling related shapes.**

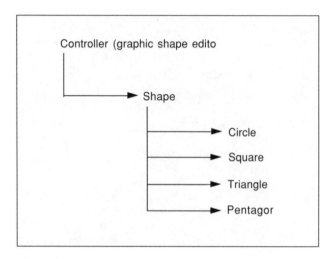

Figure 3.3 **You can add a new shape to the system without changing the shape controller.**

Once you've defined a new base type, you can build from it using inheritance. When a new type inherits from a base type, the derived type gets all the characteristics and behaviors of the base type.

Inheritance allows you to reuse code without introducing bugs. Let's say you've created a base type in C++:

```
class base {
    int state1;
    int state2;
public:
    void behavior();
};
```

or in Delphi:

```
Base = class (TObject)
  State1 : integer;
  State2 : integer;
  procedure Behavior;
end;
```

Then suppose you want to build a new type derived from the existing base type. Make the derived type identical to the base type, with one exception: Extend `base` by adding a second method called `Behavior2`. You can build `derived` simply and quickly by inheriting from `base`. You don't recode anything in the derived type that you want to keep from the base type; you just add the new behavior.

In C++:

```
class derived : public base {
public:
  void Behavior2();
};
```

In Delphi:

```
Derived = class (Base)
  procedure Behavior2;
end;
```

Because `derived` inherits all the data and methods of `base`, you don't need to redefine them. You simply tell the compiler that you want to derive a new type (`derived`) from a base type (`base`) and add the new method.

Now you can send either message (`Behavior1` or *Behavior2*) to variables of the derived type, and `derived` can handle it. In C++:

```
main() {
  derived d;
  d.state1 = 1984;
  d.state2 = 1992;
  d.behavior1();
  d.behavior2();
}
```

In Delphi:

```
var
```

```
D: Derived;
With D do
  begin
    State1:= 1984;
    State2:= 1992;
    Behavior1;
    Behavior2;
  end;
```

Notice again that you don't have to pass the variables State1 and State2 to Behavior2; derived inherited knowledge of them from base.

Sketching Your Objects

Although there's no formal methodology for object-oriented design, one of your most important first steps is to make sure that you understand the object types you're creating. You can do this by sketching out the data (properties) and functionality (behaviors) for each item you think might make a good type. Jot down the data fields and methods for each type on paper or an index card. Don't worry about the low-level details of how you'll implement the fields or methods; focus on a high level. If data don't seem related to behaviors, you might need a struct or a record instead of an object. That's fine. In hybrid languages such as C++ and Delphi, you don't have to create object types unless you want to.

As you sketch out the objects, try to draw on the real-world system you're modeling, whether it's a business, a scientific application, or whatever. If there aren't any real-world components to start with, as with some of the examples presented later in this chapter, you can abstract them based on the user interface. For example, what kinds of windows will you create for user interaction? What will each window contain? Try to simplify complex objects. Imagine more and simpler ones.

When you create your list of objects, don't worry very much about the inheritance structure. It's much easier to list the objects on index cards and then see which have duplicate fields or methods. One advantage of using index cards is that you can move them around to try different approaches to creating hierarchies. Remember that inheritance should be used only when you inherit both the data and the functionality. In many cases, you'll want to use composition so that some objects are contained in others.

Reusing Code

The creation of hierarchies through inheritance makes it easier to reuse and maintain code. You save time by reusing and extending not only your own code but also code you didn't write—even if you don't have access to the source code. You can also write extensible libraries that you can pass on to others without releasing source code. You can do this by:

❑ creating abstract types

❑ creating types that are general enough to allow themselves to be extended

❑ using virtual methods

❑ clearly defining an interface to these types

The separation of interface and implementation is especially important in object-oriented programming. The interface says, "This is what the class does"; the implementation says, "This is how the class works." You can compile a program using only the interface, but you can't link it. You can find out how a system works, vary the implementation as often as you like, and link it in without recompiling the entire project. This lets you extend the system by deriving related types without disrupting the working system. It also lets you describe and compile a system (prototype it) without actually writing an implementation. You can experiment with design and implementation and not pay very much for that experimentation (and fun).

In this chapter, you'll learn how to use encapsulation and inheritance to describe systems in types that represent aspects of the world. You'll develop a modeling system that you can use as a blueprint for general object type design. This system will show how types make it easier to model real-world problems. It describes a particularly interesting (and universal) aspect of the world, called *chaos*, and shows the peculiar order you can discover in chaos through the creation of strange attractors.

Choosing a First Application

The best way to learn object-oriented programming (or anything) is to experiment. Perhaps start by implementing something new instead of reimplementing an application you've written using a traditional approach. If you reimplement something you know, you probably won't be pushed to explore the relationships between the objects and will revert to traditional techniques instead of thinking in objects. So begin your OOP experiment with a small but new problem. Ideally, it should map to a model found in the real world, where the objects aren't too abstract.

For example, you might implement a game (such as chess or checkers), a simulation (a hardware simulation of a CPU or something slightly more abstract, such as a group of fractal curves), or something related to business (such as a calculator, or a project or contact manager). If the application models the real world, you have a starting point for determining what the objects should be. Throughout this book I'll suggest and outline applications that would make good first or second projects.

Checkers and Chess

Consider two board games: checkers and chess. Each game consists of related characteristics: an eight-by-eight-square board, two sets of playing pieces, rules for moving pieces, and rules for determining the end of the game. Because the games have so much in common, you can use an abstract type to create a common interface to a group of related subtypes.

One design approach is to begin with the smallest unit (a board piece) and work your way up. What are its characteristics? A board piece has a position, a set of legal moves, and a set of possible moves. Determining legal and possible moves is an action (or behavior), so these moves might fit into methods.

In C++, an abstract board piece might look like this:

```
class BoardPiece {
   int X;             // position along X axis
   int Y;             // position along Y axis
```

```
public:
  BoardPiece();            // Construct a board piece.
  ~BoardPiece();           // Destroy a board piece.
virtual void Legal_moves(); {}
virtual void Possible_moves(); {}
};
```

and like this in Delphi:

```
BoardPiece = class (TObject)
  X : integer;             { position along X axis }
  Y : integer;             { position along Y axis }
public
  procedure Legal_moves; virtual;
  procedure Possible_moves; virtual;
end;

Procedure BoardPiece.Possible_moves;
begin          { abstract }
end;

Procedure BoardPiece.Legal_moves;
begin          { abstract }
end;
```

Notice that the behaviors are abstract and thus are reimplemented by the types derived from BoardPiece. In C++, you can use the inline feature to implement default code. The code between the braces does nothing, but by declaring the behaviors in the abstract type you emphasize that each derived type must implement its own Legal_moves and Possible_moves behaviors. Delphi also has an inline feature, so you do not have to implement all methods (including abstract ones) separately from the declaration.

    In the previous object sketch, each board piece has a position (x,y) on the board and a way to determine its legal and possible moves. In checkers, a piece is a pawn or a king. In chess, a piece is a pawn, knight, bishop, rook, queen, or king. In both games, the pieces are related but have different legal and possible moves. By beginning with a generic BoardPiece, you can derive each piece without reimplementing the basic piece code. In C++, you can derive a checker pawn from the base type BoardPiece:

```
class CheckerPawn : public BoardPiece {
public:
    CheckerPawn();          // Construct a checker.
    ~CheckerPawn();         // Destroy a checker.
    void Legal_moves();     // Implement pawn's legal moves.
    void Possible_moves();  // Determine possible moves.
};
```

In Delphi:

```
CheckerPawn = class (BoardPiece)
 public
   procedure Legal_moves; virtual;
   procedure Possible_moves; virtual;
end;
```

You can reimplement Legal_moves as follows in C++:

```
CheckerPawn:: Legal_moves()
{       // Implement here.
}
```

In Delphi:

```
CheckerPawn.Legal_moves;
begin
  { Implement here. }
end;
```

CheckerKing is another board piece that reimplements Legal_moves and Possible_moves. In C++:

```
class CheckerKing : public BoardPiece {
public:
```

```
  CheckerKing();            // Construct a king.
  ~CheckerKing();           // Destroy a king.
  void Legal_moves();       // Implement king's legal moves.
  void Possible_moves();    // Determine possible moves.
};
```

In Delphi:

```
CheckerKing = class (BoardPiece)
 public
      procedure Legal_moves; virtual;
      procedure Possible_moves; virtual;
end;
```

A chess piece (a knight, for example) is just another board piece with reimplemented behaviors. In C++:

```
class Knight : public BoardPiece {
public:
  Knight();                 // Construct a knight.
  ~Knight();                // Destroy a knight.
  void Legal_moves();       // Implement legal moves.
  void Possible_moves();    // Determine possible moves.
};
```

In Delphi:

```
Knight = class (BoardPiece)
 public
      procedure Legal_moves; virtual;
      procedure Possible_moves; virtual;
end;
```

Notice that once you declare a method as virtual in C++ or Delphi.

As systems become more complex, the need to derive new types and reimplement the behaviors of types becomes more noticeable and important. Object-oriented programming's strength lies in letting you extend parts of a system without reimplementing the rest.

In the game example, you derived new related types—a simple hierarchical extension. In the shapes and traffic-controller examples, you extended the system by deriving new types without disrupting the mechanism for controlling the types (see Figures 3.4 and 3.5).

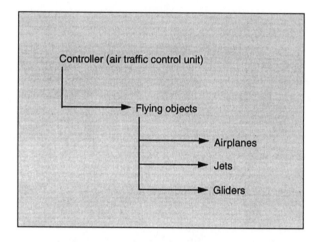

Figure 3.4 **Air traffic controller system.**

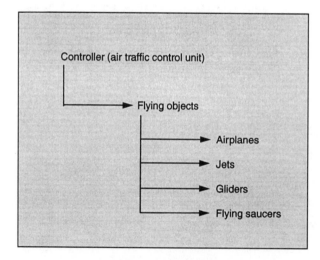

Figure 3.5 **You can add a new flying object to the system without changing the controller.**

In the next sections, you'll use these ideas to experiment. You'll explore two approaches to creating a hierarchical modeling system. One uses C++ and the other Delphi to create a form-driven modeling application. But first, some background music.

Black Art

Modeling is a black art, a way to encapsulate part of the real world in terms of the mathematical relationships among variables. You select the variables you think are important in determining changes of state in the system and then stand back and watch the action.

For example, in a two-dimensional system with variables X and Y, we might say that the current state of Y is equal to twice the current state of X (in mathematical terms, Y = 2X). In a simple linear model such as this one, you can easily visualize how the system will change from state to state: Y is always twice as big as X (see Figure 3.6).

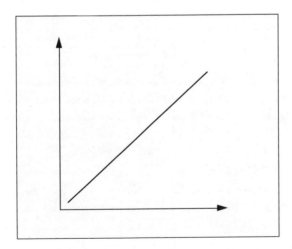

Figure 3.6 **A simple linear model: Y = 2X.**

In recent years, researchers in various fields that involve dynamics have used computers to model nonlinear systems. Because the parameters don't vary proportionally, these systems' behavior is not easily visualized or understood just by looking at numbers. The key to understanding many of these systems is to discover and study their attractors.

An *attractor* is, loosely, a state toward which a system evolves. You study attractors by looking at their pictures in a computer-generated phase, or *state*, space. In state space, a point represents all the information known about a system's state, and the space itself is a picture of the system's current state plotted against its next state (Figure 3.7).

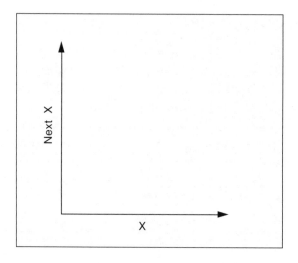

Figure 3.7 **State space.**

You want to know how the system is evolving or which state it's evolving toward. Attractors "attract" a system. As the system evolves (changes state), the collection of points representing successive states can either settle to one point (a point attractor; see Figure 3.8), repeatedly return to a group of points (a periodic attractor; see Figure 3.9), or not return to a clearly defined group of points (possibly strange; see Figure 3.10).

The system evolves as the values of the current state become the initial values of the next state. Before each loop into the next state, we plot the current system's state in state space.

Modeling systems are easily described with object-oriented techniques for several reasons:

❑ They can be abstracted easily.

❑ Every model is related to other models; they share low-level graphics primitives such as points and are plotted in space, but they differ in how they generate states.

❑ Graphics programming in general lends itself to object-oriented techniques.

❑ A model such as object-oriented programming connects the real world to the programming world.

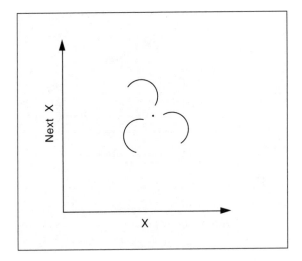

Figure 3.8 **Point attractor.**

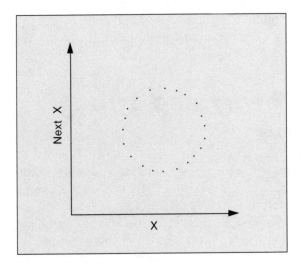

Figure 3.9 **Periodic attractor.**

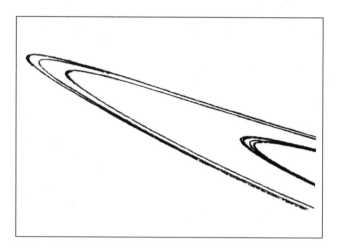

Figure 3.10 Strange attractor.

Each type (model) consists of its own characteristics, operations, and con-structors. Each uses constructors to initialize variables, types to divide the screen into multiple graphics displays, and inheritance to derive related types.

Chaos (and complexity) theory is changing the way scientists think about the evolution of dynamic systems. Because it's an excellent example of how computers have changed the way we think about the world, we'll look into its background to help you understand all the fuss about chaos. Along the way, we'll explore approaches for finding and creating types.

Chaos Theory and Strange Attractors

A dynamic system (don't confuse modeling and programming in this con-text) is anything you can describe by knowing the value of a variable whose current state depends on its previous states. The state of the sys-tem can be something you measure on a continuous scale or something with logical changes. (Is it on? Has something happened since we last checked?)

In a speech-recognition system, for example, each word in a sentence not only carries some individual weight but also affects (and is affected by) all the other words in the sentence. Consider the sentence a dynamic system that changes state through the addition of words and punctuation marks. Initially you have nothing (an empty, or "no-sentence," state). You add a word and it becomes the new sentence; add a second word and the two words are the new sentence; add a third word and the three words are the new sentence; add a punctuation mark and the three words plus punctuation are the new sentence; and so on.

When you speak, words necessarily follow one another. When you write, they follow or displace one another. Each new state represents your attempt to clarify the state of the sentence. (But each new state can either clarify or confuse, one reason parsing sentences is so difficult.) The sentence in its next state is sensitive to its current and previous states.

You could say that meanings are the attractors in the dynamic system. At any state, the sentence may have no meaning (an extinction state), one meaning (a stable state), or many meanings (possibly a chaotic state), depending on any number of things—point of view, reading or writing skill, and so on.

Mathematic Attraction

Folks from many diverse fields are trying to understand dynamic systems. Their discoveries have led to at least one conclusion: Anything whose state can change is incredibly complex.

Mathematicians and computer scientists try to wring meaning from complex systems by representing them with equations and pictures. Some particularly useful pictures exist in state space, where each point holds all the information needed to describe a dynamic system at one time.

For example, suppose a system changes state depending on a variable, such as size or number. Call the variable X and its rate of change R. Then equations such as $Nextx = R * X(* (1–X))$ can describe the system.

In this case, 1 represents unity (the entire or saturated system) and 0 represents nothing. Either extreme state (when $Nextx = 1$ or $= 0$) translates into oblivion.

The equation *Nextx = R * X(* (1–X))* is sometimes called the standard map or logistic equation, and it's been studied by mathematically inclined folks in many fields. They've discovered that it (and presumably the dynamic system it describes) behaves unpredictably. In general, any system you describe with a nonlinear equation or equations will behave unpredictably because it's extremely sensitive to initial conditions. Nearby values of *X* in one state may lead to values of *Nextx* that are far apart in the next state.

You can complicate matters even further by increasing the number of variables in a system (that is, your representation of a system). For example, two rules for changes in state—*Nextx = AX – (1–(Y*Y))* and *Nexty = BY*—can present an infinite number of states (*Nextx* values) responding to infinitely small changes in the condition of the previous state (or *X* value). This infinity of values is the chaotic set for this dynamic system.

You can see this chaos by plotting the values of each state (*Nextx*) in time. The *x*-axis is time; the *y*-axis is the value of each *X* (Figure 3.11).

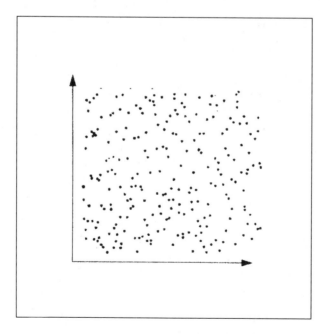

Figure 3.11 **Chaos.**

There's a certain order in most chaotic systems. One way to see this order is in state space. When we plot values of *Nextx* against values of current *X*, we uncover the attractor for the chaotic set. This attractor lives in state space and consists of all the points in the chaotic set. By mutual agreement, it's called *strange*. Figure 3.12 shows the strange attractor corresponding to the chaotic set in Figure 3.11.

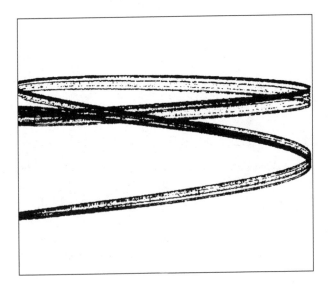

Figure 3.12 **The strange attractor corresponding to the chaotic set in Figure 3.11.**

The fractal (or self-similar) nature of the system becomes apparent when you zoom in on any area of the attractor. The deeper you go, the more complex (and detailed) the attractor becomes, yet the more orderly it appears.

Inheriting Strange Attractors

Inheritance can help describe and implement a modeling system to create and display strange attractors. Figure 3.13 shows one hierarchy for generating and displaying a model.

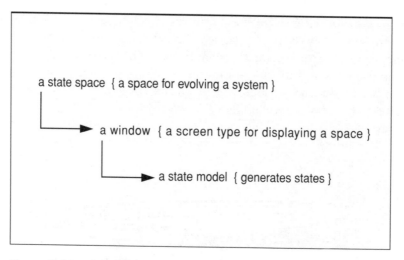

Figure 3.13 **A hierarchy for generating and displaying a model.**

Any state model will share the characteristics of having a window (a way to display evolving states) and a state space for creating state values without concern for how the space will be displayed. If you decide to reroute the generated states to something other than a window, you can easily change or bypass the window. And because the state space is independent of the display itself, you can display the space anywhere on the screen.

Display Window

A display window is characterized by four variables representing its corners and an initial point in the window. The Window constructor initializes the window, draws a border around it, and initializes a point within the window.

You might describe a window like this in C++:

```
class Window {
protected:
  int X,Y;                 // point in window
  int X1, X2, Y1, Y2;      // window location
public:
```

```
Window(int InitX, int InitY,
       int InitWinX1, int InitWinX2,
       int InitWinY1, int InitWinY2);
};
```

The display window is independent of any model and thus can be treated as a separate object type. Any model will generate values independently of the display-window specifics. These values can then be scaled into a display window.

Three likely candidates for object types are the display window, the state space, and the model generator. Each model will have a state space, where values are initially produced, and a window for displaying the scaled values.

Because a model will need to have both a display window and a state space, we can compose a model from the object types (display window and state space) or derive a model from them.

If you're a purist, you might object to deriving a model from these components; a model isn't exactly a kind of state space, nor is a state space a kind of display window. So you might compose a base model like this in C++:

```
class Model1 {
  float A,B;
public:
  Window DWindow;          // composed
  SSpace StateSpace;
  Model1(int InitWinX1, int InitWinX2,
         int InitWinY1, int InitWinY2);
  ~Model1(){};
  virtual void Generator();
};
```

One problem with this approach is that it requires you to create and manipulate three objects instead of one. A single object knows about itself, so you don't have to send messages to individual objects. Sometimes more objects are better, of course. In the remainder of this attractor example, I'll opt for impurity and derive a model from a state space and display window.

State Space

A state space is an area characterized by four range variables representing its corners and the "zoom factor" of the space. It's derived from a display window. The state-space constructor initializes the space and an initial point in the space and calls the display window to construct itself.

You might describe a state space as follows in C++:

```
class StateSpace : public Window {
protected:
  float Xpoint, Ypoint;
  float SpaceX1;                    // boundaries of space
  float SpaceX2;
  float SpaceY1;
  float SpaceY2;
public:
  StateSpace(int InitX, int InitY,
            int InitWinX1, int InitWinX2,
            int InitWinY1, int InitWinY2,
            float InitXpoint, float InitYpoint,
            float Minx, float Maxx, float Miny, float Maxy);
  void Scale();                     // scale space to window
};
```

Note that the space is independent of the display type; it's the state space of the system without any specific display characteristics.

To display the space on a screen, send a message to a display window.

Model = State Generator

A state generator creates states for the system. Its constructor also initializes its own variables and sends a message to Window to construct itself. In turn, Window sends the message to StateSpace. The generator (Model1) doesn't concern itself with any of the implementation details of Window or StateSpace; it only wants to know that a display window is open and a state space exists.

A state generator (or model) might look like this in C++:

```
class Model1 : public StateSpace {
  float A,B;
public:
  Model1(int InitWinX1, int InitWinX2,
         int InitWinY1, int InitWinY2);
  virtual void Generator();
};
```

This model generates the Henon attractor, introduced in 1976. Its implementation in C++ is:

```
void Model1::Generator() {
  setviewport(X1, Y1, X2, Y2, CLIP_ON);
  float TempX = Xpoint; // Save last state.
  float TempY = Ypoint; // Save last state.
  Xpoint = TempY + 1 - (A * TempX * TempX);    // this model
  Ypoint = B * TempX; // this model
  Scale(); // Scale new state to a window.
  putpixel(X,Y,7);
}
```

Because each model has its own space and display, you can display more than one model on the screen (as in the C++ Listing 3.1) simultaneously, or even overlap displays.

Listing 3.1 **Complete C++ Attractor**

```
// Listing 3-1.  Complete C++ attractor.
// program AttractP;
// using Borland's BGI for graphics
// substitute your own graphic driver/package
#include <graphics.h>
#include <conio.h>
#include <stdio.h>
#include <math.h>
#include <stdlib.h>
#define CLIP_ON 1
```

```
class graphics {
  int graphdriver;
  int graphmode;
  int errorcode;
public:
  // This implementation uses Borland's BGI
  graphics() { // constructor
    graphdriver = DETECT;
    initgraph(&graphdriver, &graphmode, "");
    errorcode = graphresult();
    if(errorcode != grOk) {
      printf("Graphics error: %s\n",
              grapherrormsg(errorcode));
      exit(1);
    }
  }
  ~graphics() { // clean up
    closegraph();
  }
};

class Window {
protected:
  int X,Y;                     // point in window
  int X1, X2, Y1, Y2;          // window location
public:
  Window(int InitX, int InitY,
         int InitWinX1, int InitWinX2,
         int InitWinY1, int InitWinY2);
};

class StateSpace : public Window {
protected:
  float Xpoint, Ypoint;
  float SpaceX1;               // boundaries of space
  float SpaceX2;
  float SpaceY1;
  float SpaceY2;
```

```
public:
  StateSpace(int InitX, int InitY,
              int InitWinX1, int InitWinX2,
              int InitWinY1, int InitWinY2,
              , float InitXpoint, float InitYpoint,
              float Minx, float Maxx, float Miny, float Maxy);
  void Scale();                    // scale space to window
};

class Model1 : public StateSpace {
  float A,B;
public:
  Model1(int InitWinX1, int InitWinX2,
          int InitWinY1, int InitWinY2);
  virtual void Generator();
};

class Model2 : public StateSpace {
  float R;
public:
  Model2(int InitWinX1, int InitWinX2,
          int InitWinY1, int InitWinY2);
  virtual void Generator();
};

Window::Window (int InitX, int InitY,
                int InitWinX1, int InitWinX2,
                int InitWinY1, int InitWinY2) {
  X = InitX;         // initial point in window
  Y = InitY; X1 = InitWinX1;    // window location
  X2 = InitWinX2;
  Y1 = InitWinY1;
  Y2 = InitWinY2;
  rectangle (X1, Y1, X2, Y2);
}

StateSpace::StateSpace(int InitX, int InitY,
                        int InitWinX1, int InitWinX2,
```

```
                              int InitWinY1, int InitWinY2,
                              float InitXpoint, float InitYpoint,
                              float Minx, float Maxx,
                              float Miny, float Maxy)
    : Window(InitX,InitY, InitWinX1, InitWinX2,
            InitWinY1, InitWinY2) {
    SpaceX1 = Minx; SpaceX2 = Maxx;
    SpaceY1 = Miny; SpaceY2 = Maxy;
    Xpoint = InitXpoint; Ypoint = InitYpoint;
}


void StateSpace::Scale() { // Scale point in space to window.
    X = ceil((Xpoint - SpaceX1)/(SpaceX2 - SpaceX1) * (X2 - X1));
    Y =  Y2 - (ceil((Ypoint - SpaceY1)/(SpaceY2 - SpaceY1) *
            (Y2 - Y1)));
}


Model1::Model1(int InitWinX1, int InitWinX2,
                int InitWinY1, int InitWinY2)
    : StateSpace(0,0, InitWinX1,InitWinX2, InitWinY1,InitWinY2,
                0.4,0, -1.03, 1.27, -0.3, 0.45) {
    // Set factors.
    A = 1.4;
    B = 0.3;
}


Model2::Model2(int InitWinX1, int InitWinX2,
                int InitWinY1, int InitWinY2)
    : StateSpace(0,1, InitWinX1,InitWinX2, InitWinY1,InitWinY2,
                0.4,0, -0.5, 1.0, -1, 0.5) {
    // Set factors.
    R = 4.0;
}


void Model1::Generator() {
    setviewport(X1, Y1, X2, Y2, CLIP_ON);
    float TempX = Xpoint; // Save last state.
    float TempY = Ypoint; // Save last state.
    Xpoint = TempY + 1 - (A * TempX * TempX);    // this model
```

```
    Ypoint = B * TempX; // this model
    Scale(); // Scale new state to a window.
    putpixel(X,Y,7);
}

void Model2::Generator() {
    setviewport (X1, Y1, X2, Y2, CLIP_ON);
    float Tempx = Xpoint; // Save last state.
    float Tempy = Ypoint; // Save last state.
    Ypoint = Tempx - (1 - (Tempy * Tempy));    // this model
    Xpoint = R * Tempx * (1 - Tempx);          // this model
    Scale(); // Scale point to a window.
    putpixel(X,Y,7);
}

graphics Graphics; // single global object

main() {
// Set screen and window dimensions:
    int WX1 = 0;
    int WX2 = ceil(getmaxx()/2 - 5);
    int WY1 = 0;
    int WY2 = ceil(getmaxy()/2 + 150);

// Create a model:
    Model1 M1(WX1,WX2,WY1,WY2);

// Set screen and window dimensions:
    int WWX1 = ceil(getmaxx()/2 + 5);
    int WWX2 = getmaxx();

// Create a model:
    Model2 M2(WWX1,WWX2,WY1,WY2);

    do { // Iterate the models
        M1.Generator();
        M2.Generator();
    } while (!kbhit());
}
```

Where OOP Works Best

People often wonder where object-oriented programming should be used. "Everywhere" is only a slight exaggeration—object-oriented programming is a general-purpose approach to programming. As with structured programming, there are few places where object-oriented programming is not useful.

The best applications for object-oriented programming are those that are likely to require ongoing change and are inherently complex. In fact, the more these two characteristics apply, the greater the benefits of object-oriented programming. Large, complex applications require techniques such as encapsulation and inheritance to make them manageable.

The areas where object-oriented programming are not suitable are quick and dirty programs, where it's probably not worth creating reusable objects (though you might benefit tremendously if you have a library of existing objects to build on) and low-level routines that are time-critical, such as device drivers. Otherwise, if you're developing systems or applications, you'll probably benefit from object-oriented programming. And the more you use it to build reusable objects, the greater the advantage on future projects.

A Form-Driven Delphi Strange Attractor Expert

Next, let's try a different approach to the modeling problem. This time we'll use Delphi to create a form-driven Strange Attractor Expert.

Begin as before (in the C++ example) by creating a model base for a hierarchy of models. This base model has a state space defined by four variables. A Setup procedure, common to all models in the hierarchy, initializes the scale for each model. Because each model can have its own scale, Setup can be overridden in any subclass. Similarly, each derived model will implement its own Process procedure. Process is the task; in this case, it contains the model equations for determining where to plot a graph of the model's generated points (or values). Finally, the model base contains a procedure to scale (or normalize) the results into a form:

```
ModelBase = class(TObject)
  public
    ScaleX1: Double;
    ScaleX2: Double;
    ScaleY1: Double;
    ScaleY2: Double;
    procedure Setup; virtual;
    procedure Process; virtual;
    procedure ScaleResults(var X: Double; var Y: Double; var
IntX: Integer; var IntY: Integer; Width:Integer;
Height:Integer);
  end;
```

You can then derive specific models—for example, one called ModelHenon, from the ModelBase:

```
ModelHenon = class(ModelBase)
  public
    procedure Setup;
    procedure Process(var X: Double; var Y: Double);
  end;
```

Notice that ModelHenon overrides two methods: Setup and Process.

To make a form-driven application in Delphi, you can derive a form (Tform1) from the built-in TForm Delphi class:

```
TForm1 = class(TForm)
    Button1: TButton;
    Button2: TButton;
    Button3: TButton;
    Button4: TButton;
    procedure Button1Click(Sender: TObject);
    procedure Button2Click(Sender: TObject);
```

```
    procedure Button3Click(Sender: TObject);
    procedure Button4Click(Sender: TObject);
  end;
```

This form has four buttons for running four processes: a Growth model and the Lorenz, Henon, and Rossler attractor models. Notice the pattern—properties and methods (procedures in this case) encapsulated in a class.

Don't worry very much about the details, especially if you're not a Delphi programmer. However, I think you'll find the code in Listing 3.2 pretty easy reading. Classes are declared in the interface and then implemented. Note also that the user interface (the form and its buttons) and the general operations or tasks associated with the form are all object-oriented.

Listing 3.2 **Delphi Strange Attractor Expert**

```
{ example for chapter 3, Tao of Objects 2nd edition}
{ Strange Attractor Expert }
unit Attract1;

interface

uses WinTypes, WinProcs, Classes, Graphics, Controls, Forms,
StdCtrls;

type
  TForm1 = class(TForm)
    Button1: TButton;
    Button2: TButton;
    Button3: TButton;
    Button4: TButton;
    procedure Button1Click(Sender: TObject);
    procedure Button2Click(Sender: TObject);
    procedure Button3Click(Sender: TObject);
    procedure Button4Click(Sender: TObject);
  end;

  ModelBase = class(TObject)
  public
```

```
    ScaleX1: Double;
    ScaleX2: Double;
    ScaleY1: Double;
    ScaleY2: Double;
    procedure Setup; virtual;
    procedure Process; virtual;
    procedure ScaleResults(var X: Double; var Y: Double; var
IntX: Integer; var IntY: Integer; Width:Integer;
Height:Integer);
 end;

  ModelGrowth = class (ModelBase)
   public
    procedure Setup;
    procedure Process(var X:Double; var Y:Double);
   end;

  ModelLorenz = class(ModelBase)
  public
    procedure Setup;
    procedure Process(var X: Double; var Y: Double; var
Z:Double);
   end;

  ModelHenon = class(ModelBase)
  public
    procedure Setup;
    procedure Process(var X: Double; var Y: Double);
   end;

  ModelRossler = class(ModelBase)
  public
    procedure Setup;
    procedure Process(var X:Double; var Y:Double; var Z:
Double);
   end;

  { unit variables }

var
```

```
    Form1 : TForm1;

    implementation

{$R *.FRM}

{ ModelBase }
procedure ModelBase.ScaleResults(var X: Double; var Y: Double;
var IntX: Integer; var IntY: Integer; Width: Integer; Height:
Integer);
var
   ScaledX : Double;
   ScaledY : Double;
begin
  ScaledX := (X - ScaleX1)/(ScaleX2-ScaleX1);
  ScaledY := (Y - ScaleY2)/(ScaleY1-ScaleY2);
  IntX := Round(ScaledX * Width);
  IntY := Round(ScaledY * Height);
end;

procedure ModelBase.Setup;
begin
end;

procedure ModelBase.Process;
begin
end;

{ ModelGrowth }

procedure ModelGrowth.Setup;
var
  I: Integer;
  X: Double;
  Y: Double;
begin
  ScaleX1:= 0;
```

```
  ScaleX2:= 1;
  ScaleY1 := 0;
  ScaleY2 := 1;
  X := 0.1;
  Y := 0.1;
  For I := 1 To 6000 Do
        Process(X,Y);
end;

procedure ModelGrowth.Process(var X:Double; var Y:Double);
var
   IntX:Integer;
   IntY:Integer;
   Dx : Double;
   Dy : Double;
begin
   DY := X;
   DX := 4 * X * (1 - X);

ScaleResults(X,Y,IntX,IntY,Form1.ClientWidth,Form1.ClientHeight)
;
   Form1.Canvas.Pixels[IntX,IntY] := clRed;
   X := DX;
   Y := DY;
end;

{ ModelLorenz }

procedure ModelLorenz.Setup;
var
  I: Integer;
  X: Double;
  Y: Double;
  Z: Double;
begin
  ScaleX1:= -20;
  ScaleX2:= 20;
```

```
    ScaleY1 := -10;
    ScaleY2 := 40;
    X := 0.1;
    Y := 0.1;
    Z := 0.1;
    For I := 1 To 6000 Do
            Process(X,Y,Z);
end;

procedure ModelLorenz.Process(var X: Double;var Y: Double; var
Z:Double);
var
    Dx: Double;
    Dy: Double;
    Dz: Double;
    IntX:Integer;
    IntY:Integer;
begin
    Dx := 10 * (Y-X);
    Dy := X * (28 -Z) - Y;
    Dz := X * Y - (8/3) * Z;

ScaleResults(X,Y,IntX,IntY,Form1.ClientWidth,Form1.ClientHeight)
;
    Form1.Canvas.Pixels[IntX,IntY] := clBlack;
    X := X + 0.01 * Dx;
    Y := Y + 0.01 * Dy;
    Z := Z + 0.01 * Dz;
end;

{ ModelHenon }

procedure ModelHenon.Setup;
var
    I: Integer;
    X: Double;
    Y: Double;
```

```
begin
   ScaleX1:= -1.1;
   ScaleX2:= 1.3;
   ScaleY1 := 0.45;
   ScaleY2 := - 0.3;
   X := 0.1;
   Y := 0.1;
   For I := 1 To 6000 Do
       Process(X,Y);
end;

procedure ModelHenon.Process(var X: Double; var Y: Double);
var
   IntX:Integer;
   IntY:Integer;
   Dx : Double;
   Dy : Double;
begin
   Dx := Y - 1.4 * X * X + 1 ;
   Dy := 0.3 * X;
   IntX := 0;
   IntY := 0;

ScaleResults(X,Y,IntX,IntY,Form1.ClientWidth,Form1.ClientHeight)
;
   Form1.Canvas.Pixels[IntX,IntY] := clBlue;
   X := Dx;
   Y := Dy;
end;

{ ModelRossler }

procedure ModelRossler.Setup;
var
   I: Integer;
   X: Double;
   Y: Double;
```

```
    Z: Double;
begin
  ScaleX1:= -15;
  ScaleX2:= 15;
  ScaleY1 := 70;
  ScaleY2 := -15;
  X := 0.1;
  Y := 0.1;
  Z := 0.1;
  For I := 1 To 6000 Do
        Process(X,Y,Z);
end;

procedure ModelRossler.Process(var X:Double; var Y:Double; var
Z: Double);
var
    Dx: Double;
    Dy: Double;
    Dz: Double;
    IntX:Integer;
    IntY:Integer;
begin
    Dx := -(Y + Z);
    Dy := X + (Y / 5);
    Dz := (1 / 5) + Z * (X - 5.7);
    X := X + Dx * 0.005;
    Y := Y + Dy * 0.005;
    Z := Z + Dz * 0.005;

ScaleResults(X,Y,IntX,IntY,Form1.ClientWidth,Form1.ClientHeight)
;
    Form1.Canvas.Pixels[IntX,IntY] := clGreen;
    X := X + 0.01 * Dx;
    Y := Y + 0.01 * Dy;
    Z := Z + 0.01 * Dz;
end;

procedure TForm1.Button1Click(Sender: TObject);
```

```
var
  Model : ModelGrowth;
begin
  Model := ModelGrowth.Create;
  Model.Setup;
end;

procedure TForm1.Button2Click(Sender: TObject);
var
  Model : ModelHenon;
begin
  Model := ModelHenon.Create;
  Model.Setup;
end;

procedure TForm1.Button3Click(Sender: TObject);
var
  Model : ModelLorenz;
begin
  Model := ModelLorenz.Create;
  Model.Setup;
end;

procedure TForm1.Button4Click(Sender: TObject);
var
  Model : ModelRossler;
begin
  Model := ModelRossler.Create;
  Model.Setup;
end;

begin
  RegisterClasses([TForm1, TButton]);
  Form1 := TForm1.Create(Application);
end.
```

Figures 3.14, 3.15, and 3.16 show the strange attractors generated by three of these models using the code in Listing 3.2.

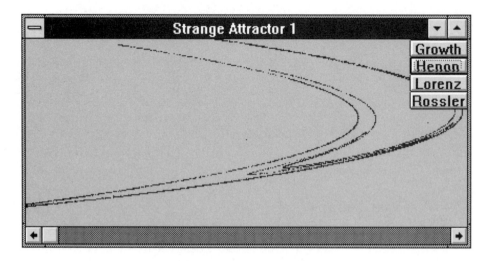

Figure 3.14 Henon attractor.

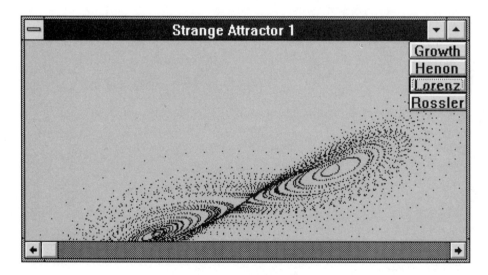

Figure 3.15 Lorenz attractor.

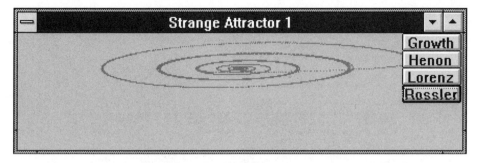

Figure 3.16 Rossler attractor.

Extending Systems

Object-oriented programming makes it easy to extend systems such as those discussed in this chapter; just add features or reimplement existing ones to create new functions. As programs become larger, they become difficult to understand, maintain, and extend. The use of types can improve understanding and help make programs easier to maintain and extend by reducing the amount of code you need to rewrite.

Object-oriented techniques can reduce confusion, improve programming efficiency, and change the way you think about the relationships between the world and your programs. Sounds good, right? So enjoy what you've learned so far and extend yourself a little more: Stand up and stretch those weary muscles before moving to the next chapter.

Chapter Four

Shaping the System

The Tao is like a well: used but never used up. It's like the eternal void: filled with infinite possibilities. It's hidden but always present.

—Lao-tzu

Since motion and change are essential properties of things, the forces causing the motion are not outside the objects, but are an intrinsic property of matter.

—Fritjof Capra

The word *polymorphism* comes from the Greek meaning "having many shapes." In object-oriented programming, you can create a type and derive new types from it using inheritance. The new derived types inherit characteristics and behaviors from their ancestors. They can also reimplement behaviors and thus change the specific behavior of a type without changing its general interface. This is polymorphism.

Programs you design using polymorphism are easy to maintain, amend, and extend because change doesn't disrupt the system. The messages you send are general; an instance's response to a message is specific.

For example, say you've created a base type in C++. You can derive new types from the existing base type (using inheritance) and allow derived types to reimplement the base type's behavior by making behaviors virtual. In C++:

```
class base {
  int state1; // private by default
public:
  virtual void SayWho();
};
```

In Delphi:

```
base = class (TObject)
private
  state1: Integer;
public
  procedure SayWho; virtual;
end;
```

Since SayWho is a virtual method, any type derived from base can reimplement SayWho however it likes. Using virtual methods, you create systems that can send general messages to any variables in a group of types. The system just sends the message; it doesn't need to know how a type will carry it out.

For example, suppose you derive two new types from a base type. In C++:

```
class derived1 : public base {
public:
  virtual; void SayWho();
};

class derived2 : public base {
public:
  virtual; void SayWho();
};
```

In Delphi:

```
Derived1 = class(Base)
public
  procedure SayWho; virtual;
end;

Derived2 = class(Base)
public
  procedure SayWho; virtual;
end;
```

Then implement `derived1` and `derived2`. In C++:

```
void derived1::SayWho(){
  cout << "I'm derived 1";
};

void derived2::SayWho(){
  cout << "I'm derived 2";
};
```

Note the use of `cout`. This predefined stream object for standard output is convenient because it simplifies output formatting. You can use `cout` to output both built-in and user-defined object types while avoiding the complications of `printf`.

Implementing `derived1` and `derived2` might look like this in a form-driven Delphi application. This code assumes that the application contains a form (`form1`) that contains a Label (`Label1`). The Label is used to display information:

```
procedure Derived1.SayWho;
begin
    Form1.Label1.Caption := 'I'm derived 1.';
end;

procedure Derived2.SayWho;
begin
    Form1.Label1.Caption := 'I'm derived 2.';
end;
```

Now you can send the `SayWho` message to both `derived1` and `derived2`, and each will respond to the message according to its implementation of SayWho.

The following piece of cereal code (not to be confused with serial or spaghetti code) illustrates polymorphism in a mouthful. For maximum enjoyment, use a debugger to trace through it. In C++:

```
// virtual functions made simple
#include <stdio.h>
#include "list.h" // list template
struct rice { // base class
  virtual void talk() {}   // common interface to types of rice
};

// different implementations for each type

struct snap : rice {
  void talk() { puts("SNAP!"); }  // inline implementation
};

struct crackle : rice {
  void talk() { puts("CRACKLE!"); }  // inline implementation
};

struct pop : rice {
```

```
    void talk() { puts("POP!"); }  // inline implementation
};

main() {
  List<rice> bowl; // A container to hold rice
  bowl.add(new pop);
  bowl.add(new crackle);
  bowl.add(new snap);
  // make an iterator to move through the bowl:
  ListIterator<rice> spoon(bowl);
  // Use the iterator to select each element:
  while(spoon.current()) {
    spoon.current()->talk(); // virtual function call
    spoon++;
  }
}
```

Note: "List h" is included in listing 4.1 later in this chapter.

The virtual function talk establishes a common interface to the various derived types of rice—Snap, Crackle, and Pop. (Rice is abstract and thus exists only as an interface to the derived types.) Thus, you can send one message—talk—and the correct behavior results.

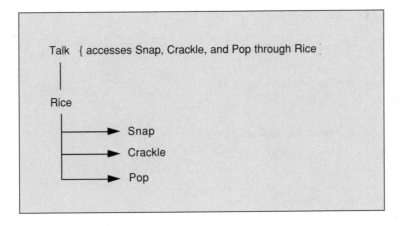

Figure 4.1 The talk **message sent to** Rice **will produce specific** Snap, Crackle, **and** Pop **behavior.**

You can create similar Rice Krispers talk in a form-driven Delphi application. Note again that we've derived a form class that contains the conveniences of buttons and display boxes. Notice also that the talk occurs during object construction in the Create constructors. In Delphi:

```
unit Rice;

interface

uses WinTypes, WinProcs, Classes, Graphics, Forms, Controls,
StdCtrls;

type
  TForm1 = class(TForm)
    Label1: TLabel;
    Button1: TButton;
    Label2: TLabel;
    Label3: TLabel;
    procedure Button1Click(Sender: TObject);
  private
    { Private declarations }
  public
    { Public declarations }
  end;

  RiceKrispers = class (TObject)
    constructor Create; virtual;
  end;

  Snap = class (RiceKrispers)
    constructor Create; virtual;
  end;

  Crackle = class (RiceKrispers)
    constructor Create; virtual;
  end;

  Pop = class (RiceKrispers)
    constructor Create; virtual;
  end;
```

```
var
  Form1: TForm1;
  Ricer: RiceKrispers;
  Snapper: Snap;
  Crackler: Crackle;
  Popper: Pop;

implementation

constructor RiceKrispers.Create;
begin
end;

constructor Snap.Create;
begin
    Form1.Label1.Caption := 'Snap';
end;

constructor Crackle.Create;
begin
    Form1.Label2.Caption := 'Crackle';
end;

constructor Pop.Create;
begin
    Form1.Label3.Caption := 'Pop';
end;

{$R *.FRM}

procedure TForm1.Button1Click(Sender: TObject);
begin
    Snapper := Snap.Create;
    Crackler := Crackle.Create;
    Popper := Pop.Create;
end;

begin
  RegisterClasses([TForm1, TLabel, TButton]);
  Form1 := TForm1.Create(Application);
end.
```

Figure 4.1 is a different kind of illustration. The talk message sent to Rice will produce specific Snap, Crackle, and Pop behavior.

Dynamics

Using polymorphism, you can take generalization a step further and send messages to any number of types (derived from a base type) without knowing how the types will behave or even what the types are. To accomplish this, you need to:

❏ Define a base type with virtual methods (a common interface)

❏ Use inheritance to derive new types

❏ Create a container/collection to hold dynamically created instances

❏ Implement a method for accessing/processing the container/collection

You're going to create dynamic types whose sizes aren't necessarily known at compile time. Let's sidestep a little and discuss how a compiler allocates memory for instances of types.

When you create an instance of a type at compile time by declaring a local variable, the compiler allocates memory for the variable on the stack at compile time. You can do that in C++ with int Number and in Delphi with Number: Integer.

You can create an instance of a type at run time (on the Delphi heap or in the C++ free-memory store) by using a pointer containing the address of a variable. In C++, you can declare a pointer to a built-in type with int* Number. In Delphi, it's NumberPtr = ^Integer.

In object-oriented programming, you can declare an instance of an object type at run time (dynamically) and simultaneously initialize it. This would be complicated if you had to do all the work; fortunately, most OOP languages do most of it for you. In C++, for example, you use the built-in operators new and delete and constructors and destructors to initialize.

For example, you can create and initialize an instance of Some Coordinates in one step. In C++, you declare a pointer to the type and assign the result of the expression new type to the pointer:

```
AnyCoordinates* SomeCoordinates = new AnyCoordinates(1,1);
```

SomeCoordinates, a pointer to the type AnyCoordinate, gets the address of a block of memory that is large enough to hold an instance of AnyCoordinates. An AnyCoordinates constructor is then called automatically to initialize an instance of AnyCoordinates with the values 1,1.

In Delphi, you might handle initialization with a slightly different approach. You can use the Create constructor to create and initialize an object:

```
{ interface }
type
      AnyCoordinates = class (TObject)
   public
      X, Y : Real;
      constructor Create;
   end;

var
   SomeCoordinates : AnyCoordinates;
{ implementation |

constructor AnyCoordinates.Create;
begin
   X := 1;
   Y := 1;
end;
```

Memory deallocation and the destruction of an instance of a type are handled in C++ by the delete operator:

```
delete Pointer_to_type;
```

Any destructor you've defined for the type is automatically called when delete executes.

In Delphi, the method Free frees memory as it destroys an instance of an object type:

```
SomeObject.Free;
```

When you define forms interactively using Delphi, you don't have to manually create or free objects. These actions are handled automatically.

However, you can perform custom initialization by overriding the automatic construction of object instances. If you manually create instances of object types, you should likewise manually free the instances when you're finished with the object.

Constructors, Destructors, and Responsibility

Constructors and destructors are used both to initialize field values and, more importantly, to allocate and deallocate memory for dynamic objects. You should write your constructors and destructors so that they take full responsibility for creating and destroying dynamic objects. This means that if an action must have occurred before a kind of object is used (for example, read a data file or reset a device), it should take place in the constructor that initializes the object. No other steps should be required to use an object because the object itself should be responsible for these matters. It also means that the construction process should in turn allocate memory for any other objects it contains.

When deallocating an object, you should deallocate any memory it uses without disposing of any objects allocated in the constructor. For example, when disposing of a linked list, you must also dispose of each node it contains. An easy way to do this is to call the destructor of each node object. This way, if the nodes themselves allocate other objects, they'll dispose of those objects in their destructor. A good general rule is that objects should allocate and deallocate the things for which they are responsible.

Managing from the Bottom Up

A linked list is an excellent data structure to use for problems involving data elements whose exact size, shape, and number aren't known at compile time. In the following two examples, one in C++ and one in Delphi, you'll define and implement a "cell manager" that processes a linked list of cells. Each cell is an instance of an object type—an object that holds a string, an integer, or a formula. The linked list is also an object type, consisting of cells and the methods needed to process the cells.

The first example is a lower-level C++ design that uses the new C++ template feature. The second example is a higher-level Delphi form-driven design that uses components (form, button, edit and label boxes) to create a user-friendly interface.

C++ Lists and Templates

Each cell can consist of any type: string, real, integer, or user-defined. See Figure 4.2.

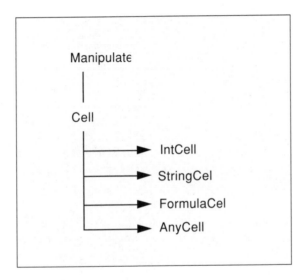

Figure 4.2 `Manipulate` **sends the cells general messages, and each cell takes care of itself.**

The cell manager can process the list without knowing exactly which type a cell contains. Each cell is an instance of a specific type and links to the next cell through a pointer. See Figure 4.3.

At the heart of the cell manager are two types: a cell and a linked list to connect cells.

A cell consists of a custom destructor (to delete the cell) and a virtual Action method for processing itself. `Cell` is the interface for a group of cells that will reimplement their own behaviors. In C++:

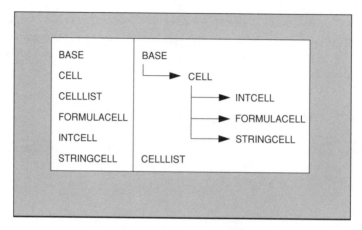

Figure 4.3 **The complete object hierarchy.**

```
class Cell {
public:
  virtual ~Cell() {}
  virtual void Action() = 0; // pure virtual function
  // each type of cell reimplements Action() appropriately
};
```

One nifty way to create a list is to use the new C++ *template* capability. A template is a code-substitution device, and it's an innovative way to reuse code. When you use inheritance, you also reuse code, but you reuse object code. A template reuses source code. In the recent old days, source code reuse was accomplished in C++ through container classes. These classes held arguments that later could be substituted for specific types. Effectively, templates move this substitution from the domain of the C++ preprocessor into the compiler. The compiler now does the work for you. (For detailed information about templates, see Bruce Eckel's excellent book, *Thinking in C++.*)

In this example, a list contains a node consisting of a pointer to a cell (or any type derived from a cell), a pointer to the next node (a link), and a constructor and destructor.

In C++:

```
template<class T>
class List {
```

```
  // nested type
  struct Node {  // The list item can be T or any
    T* Item; // class derived from T.
    Node* Next;  // Point to next node type.
    Node(T* F, Node* N) : Item(F), Next(N) {}
    ~Node() { delete Item; }
  };
  Node* Nodes;                    // points to a node.
public:
  List() : Nodes(NULL) {}         // constructor
  ~List() { // destructor
    while (Nodes) { // until end of list
      Node* N = Nodes; // Get node pointed to.
      Nodes = Nodes->Next; // Point to next node.
      delete N;       // Destroy pointer's object
    }
  }
```

You can then build a list iterator class for processing or managing the list (of cells). Note that this template is a general-purpose one and can be used with other objects in addition to cells:

```
template<class T>
class ListIterator {
  List<T>& l;
  List<T>::Node * n;
public:
  ListIterator(List<T>& L) : l(L), n(l.Nodes) {}
  T* current() {
    if(!n) return 0;
    return n->Item;
  }
  int operator++() { // prefix version
    if(n) n = n->Next;
    return int(n); // indicates end of list
  }
  int operator++(int) { // postfix version
    return operator++(); // just call prefix version
  }
};
```

The Add method adds a node—an instance of a cell or any type derived from a cell—to the list:

```
void add(T* NewItem) {      // Add an item to the list.
   Nodes = new Node(NewItem, Nodes);
  }
  friend class ListIterator<T>;
};
```

Add accepts a pointer to a cell or any type derived from a cell and can add a cell without knowing its specific type.

During the main program, each instance of the list receives a message telling it to act according to its own manipulation of the Action method. Here's the list iteration part of main():

```
// create an iterator to move through AList:
  ListIterator<Cell> it(AList);
  while (it.current()) {
    it.current()->Action();
    it++; // call to overloaded operator
```

And here's a possible Formula class:

```
class FormulaCell : public Cell {
  char* Formula;
public:
  FormulaCell(char* V) {
    Formula = new char[strlen(V) + 1];
    strcpy(Formula,V);
  }
  ~FormulaCell() { delete Formula; }
  void Action() {
    cout << "Formula: "
         << Formula << endl; // just write the formula
```

As with Add, any object requesting an Action doesn't know how any cell will specifically implement its version of Action. It just sends general messages, and each cell takes care of itself (see Figure 4.4).

Listing 4.1 C++ Cell Manager

```
// program cells

#include <string.h>
#include <iostream.h>
#include <stdlib.h>
#include "list.h" // template container list + iterator

class Cell {
public:
  virtual ~Cell() {}
  virtual void Action() = 0; // pure virtual function
  // each type of cell reimplements Action() appropriately
};

class StringCell : public Cell {
  char* Value;
public:
  StringCell(char* V) {
    Value = new char[strlen(V) + 1];
    strcpy(Value,V);
  }
  ~StringCell() { delete Value; }
  void Action() {
    cout << "String: "
         << Value << endl; // just write the string
  }
};

class IntCell : public Cell {
  int Number;
public:
  IntCell(int V) { Number = V; }
  void Action() {
    cout << "Number: "
         << Number << endl; // just write the integer
  }
};
```

```
class FormulaCell : public Cell {
  char* Formula;
public:
  FormulaCell(char* V) {
    Formula = new char[strlen(V) + 1];
    strcpy(Formula,V);
  }
  ~FormulaCell() { delete Formula; }
  void Action() {
    cout << "Formula: "
         << Formula << endl; // just write the formula
  }
};

main() {
  List<Cell> AList; // Create a list to hold cell pointers

  while(1) {
    const sz = 100;
    char S[sz];
    cout << "Enter cell value, ~ to end: ";
    cin.getline(S,sz);
    if (S[0] == '~') break; // out of while loop
    // Add instances of cell by evaluating input.
    // Determine type from first char:
    switch (S[0]) {
      case '#': // leading # indicates a formula
            AList.add(new FormulaCell(&S[1]));
            break;
      case '1': case '2': case '3': case '4':
      case '5': case '6': case '7': case '8':
      case '9': case '0':  // it's a number
            AList.add(new IntCell(atoi(S)));
            break;
      default: // otherwise, it's a string
            AList.add(new StringCell(S));
    }
  }
```

```
  // create an iterator to move through AList:
  ListIterator<Cell> it(AList);
  while (it.current()) {
    it.current()->Action();
    it++; // call to overloaded operator
  }
}


// list.h

// LIST.H
// General-purpose template container & iterator classes:
#ifndef LIST_H_
#define LIST_H_

template<class T>
class List {
  // nested type
  struct Node {  // The list item can be T or any
    T* Item; // class derived from T.
    Node* Next;  // Point to next node type.
    Node(T* F, Node* N) : Item(F), Next(N) {}
    ~Node() { delete Item; }
  };
  Node* Nodes;            // points to a node.
public:
  List() : Nodes(NULL) {}         // constructor
  ~List() { // destructor
    while (Nodes) { // until end of list
      Node* N = Nodes; // Get node pointed to.
      Nodes = Nodes->Next; // Point to next node.
      delete N;     // Destroy pointer's object
    }
  }
  void add(T* NewItem) {   // Add an item to the list.
    Nodes = new Node(NewItem, Nodes);
  }
  friend class ListIterator<T>;
```

```
};

template<class T>
class ListIterator {
  List<T>& l;
  List<T>::Node * n;
public:
  ListIterator(List<T>& L) : l(L), n(l.Nodes) {}
  T* current() {
    if(!n) return 0;
    return n->Item;
  }
  int operator++() { // prefix version
    if(n) n = n->Next;
    return int(n); // indicates end of list
  }
  int operator++(int) { // postfix version
    return operator++(); // just call prefix version
  }
};
#endif LIST_H_
```

Delphi Form-Driven Cell Manager

The next example creates a similar cell manager in Delphi but at a somewhat higher level. This cell manager derives a new form class from the
built-in TForm class, containing a button, a label, and an edit box:

```
TForm1 = class(TForm)
    Button1: TButton;
    Edit1: TEdit;
    Label1: TLabel;
    procedure Button1Click(Sender: TObject);
  private
    { Private declarations }
  public
    { Public declarations }
  end;
```

This Delphi cell manager is event-driven, so the user will control the cell manager through the button (button1).

Each cell class is derived from a base class. In this case, each cell is derived from the built-in TObject (base) class. Here's the string cell (TStringClass):

```
TStringClass = class (TObject)
   MyString: string;
   constructor Create(S: string);
   procedure Action;
  end;
```

Here's the integer cell (TIntegerClass):

```
TIntegerClass = class (TObject)
   MyString: string;
   constructor Create(S: string);
   procedure Action;
  end;
```

Here's the formula cell (TFormulaClass):

```
TFormulaClass = class (TObject)
   MyString: string;
   constructor Create(S: string);
   procedure Action;
  end;
```

The first part of the Button1Click event creates a list (using the built-in TList type), gets the user input from an edit box, reads the first character, and then evaluates it:

```
procedure TForm1.Button1Click(Sender: TObject);
var
  S : String;
  CurrentChar : Char;
  MyList: TList;
  MyIntegerObject: TIntegerClass;
```

```
  MyStringObject: TStringClass;
  MyFormulaObject: TFormulaClass;
begin
  MyList := TList.Create;          { create a list for objects }
  S := Edit1.Text;                 { get user input from an edit box }
  CurrentChar := S[1];             { read the first char to identify
}
    { evaluate here, see complete listing }
```

After the evaluation, we create an instance of the correct cell and add the new object to the list. For example, here's the result of an Integer evaluation:

```
'1','2','3','4','5','6','7','8','9','0' :
  begin
    MyIntegerObject := TIntegerClass.Create(S);
    { create a class instance }
    MyList.Add(MyIntegerObject);        { add instance to list }
  end;
```

Later in the Button1Click event procedure, the first item in the list is evaluated and the current cell object's Action method gets a message. Then the memory for the cell is freed:

```
{ Does this cell contain an Integer ? }
  If MyIntegerObject = TIntegerClass(MyList.Items[0]) then
  { get first element in list }
  begin
    MyIntegerObject.Action;
    MessageDlg(MyIntegerObject.MyString, mtInformation, [mbOk],
0); { show it }
    MyIntegerObject.Free;
    { clean up! }
  end;
```

Listing 4.2 shows the complete form-driven Delphi cell manager.

Listing 4.2 **Delphi Cell Manager**

```
unit Cellman;

interface

uses WinTypes, WinProcs, Classes, Graphics, Forms, Controls,
MsgDlg,
  StdCtrls;

type
  { the form class with controls
  to manage input/output for cell objects }

  TForm1 = class(TForm)
    Button1: TButton;
    Edit1: TEdit;
    Label1: TLabel;
    procedure Button1Click(Sender: TObject);
  private
    { Private declarations }
  public
    { Public declarations }
  end;

type
    { all cell classes are derived from
    the TObject base class }
  TStringClass = class (TObject)
    MyString: string;
    constructor Create(S: string);
    procedure Action;
  end;

  TFormulaClass = class (TObject)
    MyString: string;
    constructor Create(S: string);
    procedure Action;
```

```
    end;

    TIntegerClass = class (TObject)
      MyString: string;
      constructor Create(S: string);
      procedure Action;
    end;

var
  Form1: TForm1;

implementation

{$R *.FRM}

{ all constructors in this example
simply assign the string to a var;
in a more realistic example, you'd
do something more interesting here }

constructor TStringClass.Create(S: string);
begin
  MyString := S;
end;

constructor TFormulaClass.Create(S: string);
begin
  MyString := S;
end;

constructor TIntegerClass.Create(S: string);
begin
  MyString := S;
end;

procedure TStringClass.Action;
begin
  Form1.Label1.Caption := 'I am a string.';
```

```
end;

procedure TFormulaClass.Action;
begin
  Form1.Label1.Caption := 'I am a formula.';
end;

procedure TIntegerClass.Action;
begin
  Form1.Label1.Caption := 'I am an integer.';
end;

procedure TForm1.Button1Click(Sender: TObject);
var
  S : String;
  CurrentChar : Char;
  MyList: TList;
  MyIntegerObject: TIntegerClass;
  MyStringObject: TStringClass;
  MyFormulaObject: TFormulaClass;
begin
  MyList := TList.Create;         { create a list for objects }
  S := Edit1.Text;                   { get user input from an
edit box }
  CurrentChar := S[1];            { read the first char to iden-
tify }
  Case CurrentChar of
  '#' :                                     { # marks a
formula }
  begin
    MyFormulaObject := TFormulaClass.Create(S);  { create a
class instance }
    MyList.Add(MyFormulaObject);                    { add
instance to list }
  end;
  '1','2','3','4','5','6','7','8','9','0' :
  begin
    MyIntegerObject := TIntegerClass.Create(S);  { create a
```

```
class instance }
    MyList.Add(MyIntegerObject);          { add instance to list }
  end;
  Else
    MyStringObject := TStringClass.Create(S);
                                          { create a class instance }
    MyList.Add(MyStringObject);           { add instance to list }
  end;

  { evaluate the first item (cell) in the list }
  { clean up is just a reminder that you do
  need to clean up lists. In a more practical
  example, you'd clean up after you no longer
  needed the list }

  { Does this cell contain an Integer ? }
  If MyIntegerObject = TIntegerClass(MyList.Items[0]) then
{ get first element in list }
  begin
    MyIntegerObject.Action;
    MessageDlg(MyIntegerObject.MyString, mtInformation, [mbOk],
0); { show it }
    MyIntegerObject.Free;          { clean up! }
  end;

  { a string ?}
  If MyStringObject = TStringClass(MyList.Items[0]) then
{ get first element in list }
  begin
    MyStringObject.Action;
    MessageDlg(MyStringObject.MyString, mtInformation, [mbOk],
0); { show it }
    MyStringObject.Free;           { clean up! }
  end;

  { a formula }
  If MyFormulaObject = TFormulaClass(MyList.Items[0]) then { get
first element in list }
```

```
  begin
     MyFormulaObject.Action;
     MessageDlg(MyFormulaObject.MyString, mtInformation, [mbOk],
0); { show it }
     MyFormulaObject.Free;                 { clean up! }
  end;
     MyList.Free;
end;

begin
  RegisterClasses([TForm1, TButton, TEdit, TLabel]);
  Form1 := TForm1.Create(Application);
end.
```

Some Advantages

Object-oriented programming techniques have significantly increased programmers' potential to create more complex and dynamic programs. In particular, it's much easier to get a prototype up and running quickly than in conventional structured languages. And, in theory at least, an object-oriented program should be easier to maintain.

By considering a program a hierarchy of types and thinking of the general (or abstract) case when solving problems, you can increase your productivity. Inheritance hierarchies are conceptually simple and flexible. Programs designed to use polymorphism and dynamic techniques are potentially quite powerful and extensible.

In C++, Delphi, dBASE for Windows, and other robust OOP languages, the ability to create and destroy variables (and objects) is considered so important that it's an integral part of these languages. When you create a user-defined data type, you can easily make a dynamic variable of that type.

This means that you can build object-oriented applications that don't need to know the number or types of objects involved in a problem before they begin to solve it. This is conceptually attractive in a world where we seldom know all the tools we need to use when we begin working on a project. OOP lets us more readily adapt to unexpected situations.

Chapter Five

Dynamic Style

Blunt your sharpness, untie your knots, soften your glare, settle your dust.

—Lao-tzu

The use of polymorphic types is fundamental to object-oriented programming. A type is polymorphic if it uses virtual methods and has a method whose name is shared by more than one type in the hierarchy.

For example, in a hierarchy of musical scales, the method name `Play_minor_scale` can be shared by all musical keys. Each key actually implements its minor scale using different notes, but the message `Play_minor_scale` can be carried out without the sender's knowing the specifics of each key's implementation (see Figure 5.1).

143

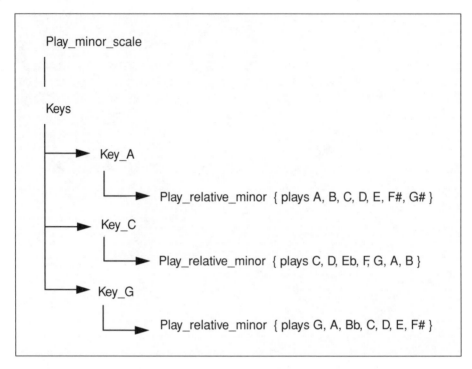

Figure 5.1 **The message** Play_minor_scale **can be carried out without the sender's knowing the specifics of each key's implementation**

Although you can create an instance of a polymorphic object type on the stack without using pointers, creating an instance at run time is convenient and useful. You can do this in C++ by allocating the instance in the free-memory store using the new and delete operators.

To create an instance of a dynamic variable in C++, you pass new the type to be created:

```
new(Shape);
```

As with C++ structs, new allocates enough space on the free-memory store for an instance of the pointer's base type and returns that space's address via the pointer. If the dynamic variable contains any virtual methods, you must use a constructor to initialize the type before sending any messages to the object. In C++, you can allocate space and initialize the instance of the type in one call:

```
Circle *ThisCircle = new Circle(140, 75, 50); // points and radius
```

Dynamic variables are useful because you can add any number of instances of them at run time without knowing the exact number of instances at compile time. By delaying system-determining decisions until run time, you disconnect code from a type's details, and the system becomes more flexible. A working system can be modified and adjusted long after it's "finished," and you can add instances of new types to the system without disrupting it.

Returning to the minor scale example, you can add a new key to the system by deriving it from Keys. Then let each descendent implement the Play_minor_scale behavior in its own way. In C++:

```
class Keys {
public:
    Keys(); {}
    ~Keys(); {}
    virtual void Play_minor_scale(); {} // will be reimplemented
                                        // by ancestors
};

class Key_F : Public Keys {
public:
    Key_F(); {}
    ~Key_F(); {}
    void Play_minor_scale(); // implement specific behavior
};
```

In Delphi:

```
Keys = class (TObject)
    procedure Play_minor_scale: virtual;
end;

Key_F = class(Keys)
    procedure Play_minor_scale; virtual;
end;
```

The next two examples, in C++ and Delphi, show how to create frame-based expert systems. Both examples use lists to maintain a set of polymorphic objects. The C++ example is fairly low-level, creating the linked list from scratch. The Delphi example is higher level and form-driven, and it derives a list from the built-in `TList` object.

Note that `Frame` is simply a synonym (in the artificial intelligence world) for a type consisting of characteristics and behaviors.

Expert Systems

Expert systems lend themselves particularly well to object-oriented programming techniques. These systems let nonexperts do the work of experts, simplify complex operations, and automate repetitive processes. Through a knowledge base of expert information, expert systems map the input characteristics and behaviors of a system, problem, pattern, or object. Input characteristics and behaviors represent colors, sizes, processes, events, symptoms, and so on. Output represents a solution, advice, pattern match, decision, report, and so on. Figure 5.2 illustrates this idea.

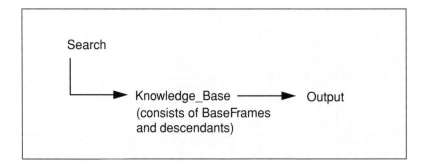

Figure 5.2 Expert systems map the input characteristics and behaviors of a system, problem, pattern, or object.

The information in an expert system's knowledge base is put there by an expert who has skill or knowledge in a specific domain. This information is almost certainly dynamic—needing to be updated and corrected as the world changes. A new expert, for example, might contribute new information. The system itself might generate new information or even correct itself. What this means for developers is that an expert system should be built so that it can evolve easily.

An expert system's inference engine can map input characteristics to output behavior in two ways, usually referred to as `backward chaining` and `forward chaining`.

A backward chaining model reasons from known results back toward the current state of the world (or system). For example, a set of symptoms might chain back to a disease having those symptoms. The system finds a match by selecting a disease and asking whether the user has the symptoms of that disease. In an *Or-based* system (`Symptom1` or `Symptom2`), a single symptom usually produces a match. In an *And-based* system (`Symptom1` and `Symptom2`), all symptoms must be present to produce a match. The system works from a disease back to the symptoms until it finds a disease that matches.

A forward chaining system reasons from the current state of the world (or system) toward a result or solution. For example, you might inform the system of your symptoms first and ask it to find the correct disease.

In this chapter, you'll construct a simple forward chaining model whose knowledge base consists of frames. You'll use the key elements of OOP to:

- ❏ create instances of object types at run time
- ❏ modify a type's behavior and derive new types without disrupting the working system
- ❏ maintain a hierarchy of objects in a linked list
- ❏ modify the mechanisms that handle the objects without disrupting existing object types

You can, for example, continue to use the list machinery and change the knowledge base to hold other types of information. The list handler doesn't need to know which object types it's sending messages to; it just sends messages and the objects handle themselves. Thus, you can let any type determine whether it's the correct one in the knowledge base to produce output for the system.

OOP in AI

Object-oriented programming is used extensively in artificial intelligence applications ranging from expert systems to pattern-recognition programs, diagnostic programs, learning applications, natural language parsers, and neural networks. Traditionally, AI work has been done using specialized languages such as LISP and Prolog. LISP was developed in the 1950s and is based on the manipulation of lists of symbols. It doesn't make a distinction between code and data, so programs themselves are lists of special symbols that define functions. LISP is considered a flexible language, but it's also primitive; it has few built-in types or functions.

Prolog emerged in the 1980s as the preferred way of doing AI programming in Europe. It's based on the idea of logic programming, in which programs query or manipulate a database of facts and rules. This higher-level language is very good at implementing expert systems because it contains a built-in inference engine for resolving complex queries.

Not surprisingly, object-oriented versions of LISP and Prolog have been developed. LISP-based languages that have objects include Loops, Flavors, Xlisp, and CLOS. Xlisp, one of the most affordable LISP implementations, is freely distributed by its author, David Betz, and is available for almost all computers. Several object-oriented variations of Prolog are (and have been) available; the most widely used is Prolog++.

Despite their flexibility for AI applications, LISP and Prolog are not widely used outside of research areas. For many programmers, C++ and Delphi are more efficient, though perhaps not as flexible, for AI programming.

Frames vs. Objects

Some AI languages implement a more flexible type of frame that has many of the same characteristics of objects. Think of a frame as consisting of "slots" that contain facts. You can use frames to derive "fuzzy knowledge" based on rules stored in the frames themselves. For example, you could describe animals through frames that explain some of the default characteristics and provide rules for determining information that's not directly stored.

In one case, you might have a `Marsupial` frame that has slots for what they eat and where they live. The facets for these slots could specify that the default values are `Kangaroo` and `In Australia`. You could also have a special slot called `AKO` for "a-kind-of." You could use this to say that a `Kangaroo` is a kind of `Marsupial`. This gives a kind of inheritance between `Kangaroo` and `Marsupial` frames. In very flexible frame-based systems, the rules for evaluating slots and the relationships between frames can be changed dynamically at run time.

Finding the Objects

Let's begin the C++ expert system/frame example by envisioning the kinds of types we need. When you design a system around types, try to think simply first and extend your ideas later. The more you think in the abstract, the better.

This expert system will consist of a template of characteristics to evaluate (input characteristics), an inference engine (rules for mapping input to output), a knowledge base of expert information (which the inference engine will use to infer output), and output behaviors (results/reports).

First, create an abstract `BaseFrame`, the base type for this expert system. `BaseFrame` will consist of a constructor, a destructor, and methods that will be shared by all derived types. `BaseFrame` is the ancestor for the frames derived from it. In C++:

```cpp
class BaseFrame {
  enum { sz = 100 };
  char id[sz];
public:
  BaseFrame() { memset(id, 0, sz); } // zero buffer
  virtual ~BaseFrame() {}
  // Get input characteristics for comparison from a stream:
  virtual void input(istream&) = 0; // pure virtual function
  // Evaluate input characteristics:
  virtual void eval() = 0;
  virtual void output() = 0; // Determine output behavior
  const char* name() { return id; } // read the name
```

```
// write the name:
void name(const char* nm) { strncpy(id, nm, sz - 1); }
};
```

To keep this expert system pertinent, let's say it contains information about sports teams and the behaviors for getting input and determining correct output. The correct output might correspond to predictions about how well this team is expected to do in its next game.

SportsFrame, then, is an object type containing information about a sports team. In C++:

```
class SportsFrame : public BaseFrame {
protected:
        int Total_points;
        int Points_against;
        int Wins;
        int Losses;
        int Cur_Tp;
        int Cur_Pa;
        int Cur_W;
        int Cur_L;

        SportsFrame(char * id int I1, int I2, int I3, int I4)
          { name (id);Total_points = I1;
            Points_against = I2;
            Wins = I3;
            Losses = I4;
          }
        ~SportsFrame();
        void input();
        void eval();
        void output();
};
```

SportsFrame has eight characteristics—Cur_Tp, Cur_Pa, Cur_W, Cur_L, Total_points, Points_ against, Wins, and Losses—but you can easily add more, either by adding variables to SportsFrame or by deriving a new type from BaseFrame.

The current input (Cur_tp, Cur_pa, Cur_w, and Cur_l) is also encapsulated in SportsFrame, allowing each SportsFrame to have its own input. BaseFrame is general and could represent anything from a simple lookup system to an advisory system to a real-time system that receives input from devices. To create a guage, for example, you might derive GaugeFrame from BaseFrame and add variables to represent such characteristics as temperature, pressure, and flow.

You'll need to decide how to store and access each frame derived from BaseFrame. Remember, you want the system to be as flexible as it can be and to grow and evolve. The most flexible structure for handling unknown growth is a collection (a list, for example). Recall the one you created in Chapter 4. It used a template and a list iterator. In C++:

```
template<class T>
class List {
  // nested type
  struct Node {  // The list item can be T or any
    T* Item; // class derived from T.
    Node* Next;  // Point to next node type.
    Node(T* F, Node* N) : Item(F), Next(N) {}
    ~Node() { delete Item; }
  };
  Node* Nodes;              // points to a node.
public:
  List() : Nodes(NULL) {}          // constructor
  ~List() { // destructor
    while (Nodes) { // until end of list
      Node* N = Nodes; // Get node pointed to.
      Nodes = Nodes->Next; // Point to next node.
      delete N;      // Destroy pointer's object
    }
  }
  void add(T* NewItem) {   // Add an item to the list.
    Nodes = new Node(NewItem, Nodes);
  }
  friend class ListIterator<T>;
};
```

The complete List implementation is shown in Listing 5.1.

The three keys to making this system flexible are inheritance, which lets you modify BaseFrame by deriving new types from it; polymorphism, which lets the same name represent different behaviors; and dynamic memory allocation, which lets you create instances of BaseFrames and types derived from BaseFrame at run time. The interface to the different implementations stays the same.

The more general an object type, the easier it is to extend. The input, evaluation, and output methods for BaseFrame are all virtual, so you can derive new frames and reimplement any or all of a frame's behaavior.

In this example, SportsFrame implements its evaluation behavior in terms of an And rule. In other words, a SportsFrame produces an output if two of its existing characteristics match the current state of those charactristics. In C++:

```
void SportsFrame::eval() {          // evaluation AND;

if ((Cur_Tp == Total_points)
     && (Cur_Pa == Points_against))
     output();
};
```

You can easily dereive a new frame from SportsFrame to implement another rule (Or, for example). In C++:

```
class OrFrame : public SportsFrame {
     public:
     OrFrame(char * id int I1, int I2, int I3, int I4):
     SportsFrame(I1,I2,I3,I4){name(id);}
     void eval();
};

void OrFrame::eval() {                // Implement OR.

     if ((Cur_Tp == Total_points)
        || (Cur_Pa == Points_against)
        || (Cur_W == Wins)
```

```
            || (Cur_L == Losses))
        output();
};
```

You can add instances of SportsFrames and OrFrames to a single list (a single system) and thus implement both And and *Or* rules simultaneously. The following code constructs and adds two SportsFrames and one OrFrame to the same list. It then iterates through the list. In C++:

```
main() {
  // Create a List to hold BaseFrame pointers:
  List<BaseFrame> AList;

  // Create and add knowledge frames to a list.
  AList.add(new SportsFrame("bob", 75, 82, 1, 5));
  AList.add(new SportsFrame("alice", 51, 82, 6, 3));
  AList.add(new OrFrame("john", 86, 84, 7, 2));

  // Input to BaseFrames and descendants from file:
  ifstream data("sports.dat");
  ListIterator<BaseFrame> it(AList);
  while (it.current()) {
    it.current()->input(data);
    it++; // call to overloaded operator
  }

  // Traverse list, display frames in expert system, and
  // evaluate.
  ListIterator<BaseFrame> it2(AList);
  while (it2.current()) {
    it2.current()->output();
    cout << "evaluating:" << endl;
    it2.current()->eval();
    it2++; // call to overloaded operator
  }
}
```

The complete C++ frame-based expert system is shown in Listing 5.1.

Listing 5.1 And/Or **Frame-Based Expert System in C++**

```cpp
// Listing 5-1.  And/or frame-based expert system in C++.
#include <fstream.h> // for stream input and output
#include <string.h>
#include "list.h" // template container list + iterator

// class hierarchy
class BaseFrame {
  enum { sz = 100 };
  char id[sz];
public:
  BaseFrame() { memset(id, 0, sz); } // zero buffer
  virtual ~BaseFrame() {}
  // Get input characteristics for comparison from a stream:
  virtual void input(istream&) = 0; // pure virtual function
  // Evaluate input characteristics:
  virtual void eval() = 0;
  virtual void output() = 0; // Determine output behavior
  const char* name() { return id; } // read the name
  // write the name:
  void name(const char* nm) { strncpy(id, nm, sz - 1); }
};

class SportsFrame : public BaseFrame {
protected:
  int Total_points;
  int Points_against;
  int Wins;
  int Losses;
  int Cur_Tp;
  int Cur_Pa;
  int Cur_W;
  int Cur_L;
public:
  SportsFrame(char * id, int I1, int I2, int I3, int I4) {
    name(id);
    Total_points = I1;
```

```
    Points_against = I2;
    Wins = I3;
    Losses = I4;
  }
  void input(istream&);
  void eval();
  void output();
};

void SportsFrame::input(istream& is) {
  is >> Cur_Tp;
  is >> Cur_Pa;
  is >> Cur_W;
  is >> Cur_L;
}

void SportsFrame::output() {
  cout << name() << ":" << endl;
  cout << "Current Points = " << Cur_Tp << endl;
  cout << "Current Against = " << Cur_Pa << endl;
  cout << "Current Wins = " << Cur_W << endl;
  cout << "Current Losses = " << Cur_L << endl;
}

void SportsFrame::eval() {        // evaluation AND;
  if ((Cur_Tp == Total_points)
      && (Cur_Pa == Points_against)) {
    cout << "match" << endl;
    output();
  }
}

class OrFrame : public SportsFrame {
public:
  OrFrame(char * id, int I1, int I2, int I3, int I4)
    : SportsFrame(id, I1,I2,I3,I4)
  { name(id); }
  void eval();
```

```
};

void OrFrame::eval() {                // Implement OR.
  cout << "evaluating: " << name() << endl;
  if ((Cur_Tp == Total_points)
      || (Cur_Pa == Points_against)
      || (Cur_W == Wins)
      || (Cur_L == Losses)) {
      cout << "match" << endl;
      output();
  }
}

main() {
  // Create a List to hold BaseFrame pointers:
  List<BaseFrame> AList;

  // Create and add knowledge frames to a list.
  AList.add(new SportsFrame("bob", 75, 82, 1, 5));
  AList.add(new SportsFrame("alice", 51, 82, 6, 3));
  AList.add(new OrFrame("john", 86, 84, 7, 2));

  // Input to BaseFrames and descendants from file:
  ifstream data("sports.dat");
  ListIterator<BaseFrame> it(AList);
  while (it.current()) {
    it.current()->input(data);
    it++; // call to overloaded operator
  }

  // Traverse list, display frames in expert system, and
  // evaluate.
  ListIterator<BaseFrame> it2(AList);
  while (it2.current()) {
    it2.current()->output();
    cout << "evaluating:" << endl;
    it2.current()->eval();
    it2++; // call to overloaded operator
```

```
  }
}

// LIST.H
// General-purpose template container & iterator classes:
#ifndef LIST_H_
#define LIST_H_

template<class T>
class List {
  // nested type
  struct Node {  // The list item can be T or any
    T* Item; // class derived from T.
    Node* Next;  // Point to next node type.
    Node(T* F, Node* N) : Item(F), Next(N) {}
    ~Node() { delete Item; }
  };
  Node* Nodes;              // points to a node.
public:
  List() : Nodes(NULL) {}         // constructor
  ~List() { // destructor
    while (Nodes) { // until end of list
      Node* N = Nodes; // Get node pointed to.
      Nodes = Nodes->Next; // Point to next node.
      delete N;      // Destroy pointer's object
    }
  }
  void add(T* NewItem) {   // Add an item to the list.
    Nodes = new Node(NewItem, Nodes);
  }
  friend class ListIterator<T>;
};

template<class T>
class ListIterator {
  List<T>& l;
  List<T>::Node * n;
public:
```

```
ListIterator(List<T>& L) : l(L), n(l.Nodes) {}
T* current() {
  if(!n) return 0;
  return n->Item;
}
int operator++() { // prefix version
  if(n) n = n->Next;
  return int(n); // indicates end of list
}
int operator++(int) { // postfix version
  return operator++(); // just call prefix version
}
};
#endif LIST_H_
```

And/Or Frame-Based, Form-Driven Expert System in Delphi

A form-driven Delphi version of the previous frame-based expert system
works similarly. It's a bit more complex-looking because it includes a complete user interface. As in previous chapters, derive a form from the class
TForm:

```
type
  TForm1 = class(TForm)
    Button1: TButton;
    Label1: TLabel;
    Label2: TLabel;
    Label3: TLabel;
    Label4: TLabel;
    Label5: TLabel;
    Memo1: TMemo;
    procedure Button1Click(Sender: TObject);
  private
    { Private declarations }
  public
```

```
  { Public declarations }
end;
```

This new class includes a button to allow the user to control the form, five labels for reporting frame information, and memo box (a fancy textbox) to display frame matches.

The frame hierarchy begins with a BaseFrame class derived from the built-in Delphi TObject class:

```
{ frame hierarchy }
BaseFrame = class (TObject)
  This_Tp : Integer;
  This_Pa: Integer;
  This_W: Integer;
  This_L: Integer;
  Cur_Tp : Integer;
  Cur_Pa : Integer;
  Cur_W: Integer;
  Cur_L: Integer;
  procedure Input; virtual;
  procedure Eval; virtual;
  procedure SetCurrent(I1,I2,I3,I4: Integer);
  procedure Output; virtual;
  procedure Report;
end;
```

SportsFrames (which have And rule behavior) and OrFrames are derived from BaseFrame:

```
SportsFrame = class (BaseFrame)
public
  constructor Create(I1,I2,I3,I4: Integer);
  procedure Eval; virtual;
  procedure Id;
end;

OrFrame = class (BaseFrame)
  constructor Create(I1,I2,I3,I4: Integer);
```

```
  procedure Id;
  procedure Eval; virtual;
end;
```

The complete Delphi frame-based expert system is shown in Listing 5.2.

Listing 5.2 And/Or Frame-Based, Form-Driven Expert System in Delphi

```
unit Frame1;

interface

uses WinTypes, WinProcs, Classes, Graphics, Forms, Controls,
StdCtrls;

type
  TForm1 = class (TForm)
    Button1: TButton;
    Label1: TLabel;
    Label2: TLabel;
    Label3: TLabel;
    Label4: TLabel;
    Label5: TLabel;
    Memo1: TMemo;
    procedure Button1Click(Sender: TObject);
  private
    { Private declarations }
  public
    { Public declarations }
  end;

{ frame hierarchy }
BaseFrame = class (TObject)
  This_Tp : Integer;
  This_Pa: Integer;
  This_W: Integer;
  This_L: Integer;
  Cur_Tp : Integer;
```

```
  Cur_Pa : Integer;
  Cur_W: Integer;
  Cur_L: Integer;
  procedure Input; virtual;
  procedure Eval; virtual;
  procedure SetCurrent(I1,I2,I3,I4: Integer);
  procedure Output; virtual;
  procedure Report;
end;

SportsFrame = class (BaseFrame)
public
  constructor Create(I1,I2,I3,I4: Integer);
  procedure Eval; virtual;
  procedure Id;
end;

OrFrame = class (BaseFrame)
  constructor Create(I1,I2,I3,I4: Integer);
  procedure Id;
  procedure Eval; virtual;
end;


var
  Form1: TForm1;

implementation

{$R *.FRM}

{ BaseFrame }

  procedure BaseFrame.Input;
  begin
  end;

  procedure BaseFrame.Eval;
```

```
    begin
    end;

    procedure BaseFrame.SetCurrent(I1,I2,I3,I4:Integer);
    begin
      Cur_Tp := I1;
      Cur_Pa := I2;
      Cur_W := I3;
      Cur_L := I4;
      end;

procedure BaseFrame.Output;
var
  S,S2,S3,S4 : String;
begin
  Str(This_Tp,S);
  Str(This_Pa,S2);
  Str(This_W,S3);
  Str(This_L,S4);
  Form1.Label1.Caption := S;
  Form1.Label2.Caption := S2;
  Form1.Label3.Caption := S3;
  Form1.Label4.Caption := S4;
end;

procedure BaseFrame.Report;
begin
  Form1.Label5.Caption := 'Point Match!';
end;

{ SportsFrame }

constructor SportsFrame.Create(I1,I2,I3,I4:Integer);
begin
  This_Tp:= I1;
  This_Pa := I2;
  This_W := I3;
  This_L := I4;
```

```
end;

procedure SportsFrame.Id;
begin
  Form1.Memo1.Text := Form1.Memo1.Text + 'SportsFrame';
end;


procedure SportsFrame.Eval;
begin
  Output;
  If((Cur_Tp = This_Tp)
    And (Cur_Pa = This_Pa))
  Then
    Id;
    Report;
end;

{ OrFrame }

constructor OrFrame.Create(I1,I2,I3,I4:Integer);
begin
  This_Tp:= I1;
  This_Pa := I2;
  This_W := I3;
  This_L := I4;
end;

procedure OrFrame.Eval;
begin
  Output;
  If((Cur_Tp = This_Tp)
    Or (Cur_Pa = This_Pa)
    Or (Cur_W = This_W)
    Or (Cur_L = This_L))
  Then
    Id;
    Report;
```

```
end;

procedure OrFrame.ID;
begin
  Form1.Memo1.Text := Form1.Memo1.Text + 'OrFrame';
end;

{ button }

procedure TForm1.Button1Click(Sender: TObject);
var
  AList : TList;
  Sf : SportsFrame;
  Ofr : OrFrame;
  I : Integer;
begin
  AList := TList.Create;
  { hard code some new input;
   make this user derived in a more
  robust app }
  Sf := SportsFrame.Create(75,82,1,5);
  Sf.SetCurrent(75,82,1,5);
  Ofr := OrFrame.Create(75,75,1,5);
  Ofr.SetCurrent(75,82,5,2);
  { add to the list }
  AList.Add(Sf);
  AList.Add(Ofr);
  { move through this list }
  For I := 0 To 1 do
    If Sf = SportsFrame(AList.Items[I]) then { eval this element
in list }
      Sf.Eval;
    If Ofr = OrFrame(AList.Items[I]) then { eval this element in
list }
      Ofr.Eval;
end;

begin
```

```
RegisterClasses([TForm1, TButton, TLabel, TListBox, TMemo]);
  Form1 := TForm1.Create(Application);
end.
```

Programming for Change

Programs composed of object types are powerful and flexible because of their built-in capacity for change. Object-oriented design anticipates the evolution of real-world systems and programs. Any program of even modest complexity will change, so anticipating change is a natural process.

Change can take two forms. External changes take place in the outside world. For the system to continue modeling the outside world accurately, it must be able to change. A simple example is adding new printers or graphics terminals to a system. Adding desktop publishing features to a word-processing program is more complicated. Most programming systems (particularly structured systems) assume that all changes are external.

Internal changes take place in your understanding of a problem. Nothing has necessarily changed in the outside world; rather, your perception of the problem has changed. For example, you might rewrite an algorithm to increase its execution speed or reorganize code to improve its readability. You might also discover that three different types have features in common and decide to create an abstract base type from which to derive them.

You may discover that you can improve a type you created for a program by modifying its design. Most non–object-oriented languages assume that you understand the system completely before you begin coding and either won't make mistakes or won't learn from them. In short, non–object-oriented languages don't adapt easily to internal changes.

Object-oriented languages, on the other hand, provide techniques for creating systems that adapt easily to external and internal changes. Object-oriented design lets your ideas grow with the system. Complex projects, such as those associated with artificial intelligence, must be explorative, creative, dynamic, and experimental—requirements easily met by object-oriented languages.

Chapter
Six

OOP Design in the Real World

When you have names and forms, know that they're provisional.
                                                        —Lao-tzu

Since the first edition of *The Tao of Objects* was published in 1990, many of the major software development tools have incorporated object-oriented techniques into their designs. The idea of plug-and-play objects and components is clearly one of the "big ideas" of the mid-90s in computing. It also seems fitting that the kingpin of the mid-80s in database development has made a dramatic comeback, in part by incorporating OOP techniques into its design.

167

dBASE for Windows now includes state-of-the-art use of object-oriented technology. The dBASE for Windows GUI (graphical user interface) is based on objects. The database system, the tables, the forms, and so on that you use to develop dBASE applications are object-based. The built-in dBASE programming language is truly object-oriented.

Some database development systems, such as Paradox for Windows and Microsoft Access, are object-based. But even though object PAL, the built-in language of Paradox for Windows, is a powerful database programming language, it isn't object-oriented. On the other hand, dBASE for Windows' built-in programming language and the code generated by dBASE for Windows' built-in tools, such as the Form Expert, are object-oriented.

In the first part of this chapter, I'll explain the important differences between object-based and object-oriented programming languages. I'll show why dBASE is object-oriented (as well as object-based), and I'll show how to use its powerful object-oriented extensions to create reusable objects. In the second part of the chapter, I'll show another approach to object-oriented design using Visual Basic.

First, this chapter compares object-based and object-oriented development, focusing on OOP design with dBASE for Windows. The remainder is a hands-on demonstration of object-oriented database development. The first two applications developed here—LAUNSET and LAUNRUN—are useful dBASE for Windows applications that show how to:

❏ use built-in dBASE classes

❏ create new classes

❏ override existing class properties and behavior

❏ launch (or run) external tools or applications

❏ create custom controls

The second application also implements a database and demonstrates another powerful, if somewhat limited, approach to OOP design—Visual Basic's.

Object-Based Design and Programming

In an object-based system, such as Paradox for Windows, users implicitly and programmers explicitly treat all existing components of a system as objects. A form or a table is an object. A record is an object. Each time you create a new table or form, you create an instance of the table or form based on an existing table class or form class. In short, a prototype that you use to create specific objects is a *class*. An instance (or variable) of a class is an *object*.

However, an object-based system doesn't let you use a programming language (or design tool) to create your own classes. In an object-based system you create instances of existing classes. You can use an object as is or modify its properties. As you've learned throughout this book, in object-oriented systems, such as C++, Delphi, and dBASE for Windows, you can derive new objects from existing classes of objects, modify and manipulate those objects, and create brand new classes of objects as well.

Using Classes in dBASE for Windows

A class is a prototype for any number of objects. A class defines properties and behaviors that are shared by all objects created from the class.

Before you learn how to create your own classes, consider their use. In dBASE for Windows, you use an existing class by defining an instance (or object) of the class. For example, dBASE for Windows has a built-in class called Form. You can use this Form class by defining (or creating) your own forms based on this class. The following command (typed in the Command window) handles it:

```
DEFINE FORM ViewForm    && Create a form (an object) based on a
                        && Class (FORM)
```

To open the form, use the form's built-in Open method, as in the following command:

```
ViewForm.Open()          && Open the form
```

Notice the dot separating the object (ViewForm) and one of its methods (Open). To use (or access) an object's properties or methods, specifiy the object and the property or method you want to use or manipulate. Optionally, a method may require a parameter:

```
ViewForm.SomeMethod(AParam)
```

You can change the value of a property by using similar dot notation. The following line modifies the form's Top property:

```
ViewForm.Top = 15   && Position this form's top
```

Using classes this way is still object-based but dynamic, because you can modify the existing properties of any object based on the class. For example, any Form based on the Form class has a property called Top. You can change a Form's Top property in the Command window, in code or visually (by moving the form during design mode), and the Form (an object) will instantly reflect the change.

dBASE for Windows: Object-Based and Object-Oriented

As with C++ and Delphi, in dBASE for Windows the fun begins when you use its object-oriented capability to create your own classes. These classes can be based on predefined dBASE for Windows classes, classes in DLLs, or classes in custom control files, or you can create classes from scratch. If you derive a Class from an existing Class, the new Class you declare inherits all the properties and methods of that SuperClass. The derived Class is called a SubClass.

After you declare (or create) a class, you can define new objects based on that class. In short, you can use the classes you create just as if they were built into the dBASE system. The ability to create your own classes, which the dBASE compiler treats as if they were built-in types, is a feature that makes dBASE for Windows stand out from other database systems, including Microsoft Access and Paradox for Windows.

To create a class, use the `CLASS` and `ENDCLASS` keywords as follows:

```
CLASS INSTRUMENT
     This.NumOfStrings = 6
     This.InstrumentName = "Base Instrument"
ENDCLASS
```

In this code, `INSTRUMENT` is the name of a new class. `NumOfStrings` and `InstrumentName` are properties that every instance (or object) of the class `INSTRUMENT` will have. `This` is a keyword referring to the object created from the class, in this case, `INSTRUMENT`.

To create a hierarchy of classes based on `INSTRUMENT`, derive subclasses as follows:

```
CLASS GUITAR OF INSTRUMENT
     This.InstrumentName = "Guitar"
ENDCLASS
CLASS MANDOLIN OF INSTRUMENT
     This.NumOfStrings = 8
     This.InstrumentName = "Mandolin"
ENDCLASS
```

And so on.

Notice that any derived class—for example, `GUITAR`—inherits all the properties of its superclass, in this case `INSTRUMENT`. In addition, a class—for example, `MANDOLIN`—can override an inherited property. In the previous code snippet, `MANDOLIN` overrides both inherited properties, `NumOfStrings` and `InstrumentName`. `GUITAR` overrides `InstrumentName` but retains the inherited `NumOfStrings` value.

A subclass can also add new behavior or override the existing behavior in its superclass. For example, the following code declares a slightly different version of the INSTRUMENT class, adding a PlaySound method or (procedure):

```
CLASS INSTRUMENT
        This.NumOfStrings = 6
        This.InstrumentName = "Base Instrument"
        PROCEDURE PlaySound
            && code procedure here
            RETURN
ENDCLASS
```

The following code derives a subclass of INSTRUMENT and overrides both properties of INSTRUMENT and its PlaySound method:

```
CLASS VIOLIN OF INSTRUMENT
        This.NumOfStrings = 4
        This.InstrumentName = "Piano"
        PROCEDURE PlaySound
        && new code here
        RETURN
ENDCLASS
```

Launching an Example

To give you a hands-on feeling for how you can use object-oriented techniques in your dBASE for Windows applications, the next section details the creation of two example projects: LAUNRUN and LAUNSET. LAUNRUN is an external tool launcher, and LAUNSET sets up the launcher. *LAUNCHAIR, as Larry Fogg would say, and not created here, is a place to sit.*

Imagine that you've created several tools in another programming language to manipulate some dBASE tables. Or you simply want to launch other applications (such as Microsoft Excel or Task Manager) from within dBASE for Windows. You can easily launch these tools from dBASE Navigator by creating a tool setup form, LAUNSET, and a tool launch form, LAUNRUN.

Note: In this chapter I use a Form=Application development technique. This is an equation I've developed using my favorite all-purpose programming languages: Visual Basic and Delphi. It's also the way most popular Windows applications work. A main or startup form initiates each application. You don't have to develop dBASE for Windows applications this way. Instead you can write programs that manipulate forms. I prefer to develop as much of a project as I can "visually," using visual design tools, such as the dBASE for Windows Form Expert. When I need to, of course, I write code.

Both LAUNSET and LAUNRUN access a single table, called **Tools1.dbf**, which stores two kinds of information about an external tool: its name and its path.

In addition, both projects use a custom control class based on the built-in `Browse` class. You define and save this class in a .PRG (program) file. The LAUNSET and LAUNRUN forms (or applications) use the `#include` keyword to include this program file. In additon, each overrides a `Browse` control class event procedure.

The two applications allow you to set up and launch any external tool (or other Windows application) from dBASE Navigator. Use this design as a beginning for more intricate systems that launch external tools or Windows applications.

Figure 6.1 illustrates the object hierarchy of these two dBASE for Windows applications. The two applications are forms derived from the form class. Each new derived form contains a BR class, which is "derived" from the dBASE `Browser` class.

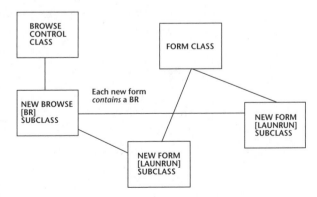

Figure 6.1 **Two applications that use (and improve on) a common class.**

Step 1: Create a Catalog

Although this step is optional, I recommend it to simplify application organization. Use Navigator to create a new Catalog called Launch. See Figure 6.2.

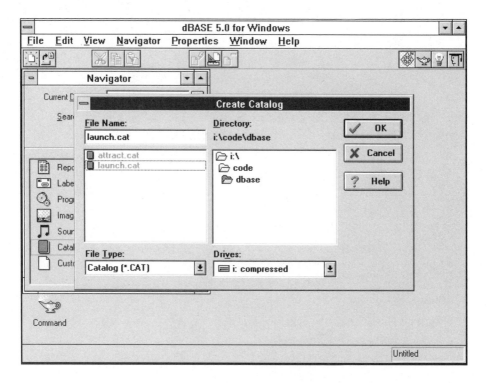

Figure 6.2 Use Navigator to create a new Catalog called Launch.

Step 2: Create a Table

Begin by creating a table, **tools1.dbf**, consisting of two character fields. Figure 6.3 shows this table in design mode.

Save the table. Close it.

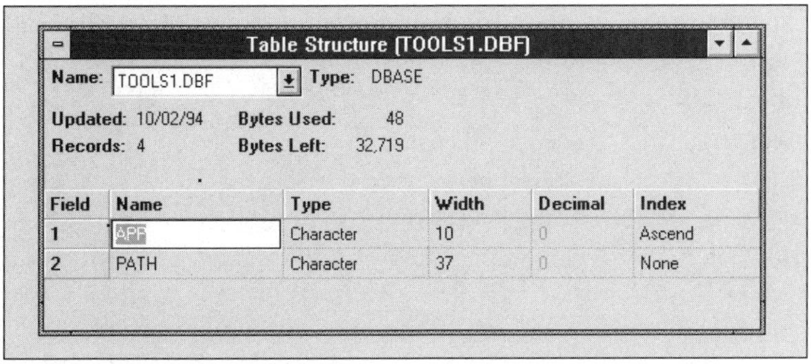

Figure 6.3 Table: tools1.dbf in design mode.

Step 3: Create a .Prg File

Before using Form Expert to create the forms for these applications, use Navigator to create a new program file to hold the new Browse class (called BR) that you want to be accessible from both applications. Save this .Prg file as **Browse1.prg**.

Edit (or design) **Browse1.prg.** Note that this file can store many classes, although the examples in this chapter require only a single new class. It's a good idea to put in separate modules (or program files) code that you want to make available to more than one application or form.

Enter the following code:

```
CLASS BR (F) OF BROWSE (F)
   Set Procedure To C:\DBASEWIN\SAMPLES\BUTTONS.CC additive
   This.Height = 7
   This.Left = 0
   This.Top = 0
   This.Width = 15.5
   This.ShowHeading = .F.
   This.ColorNormal = "N/W"
   This.ShowDeleted = .F.
   This.FontBold = .F.
   This.ShowRecNo = .F.
ENDCLASS
```

This code derives a new custom control, BR, from the Browse control that ships with dBASE for Windows. On my system, dBASE for Windows custom controls are located in C:\DBASEWIN\SAMPLES\BUTTONS.CC.

Notice that this new Browse subclass, BR, overrides several of the properties—Height, Left, etc—that it inherited from the Browse class. Any new Browse control (object) that you create from this class, BR, will have all the properties of the Browse superclass by default. In addition, you can optionally create new properties and methods (or procedures) for the derived class, BR.

Save this code.

Step 4: Create a SetUp Tools Form

Next, create and save a form as LAUNSET.WFM. An easy way to create a form is to use Form Expert. You can open Form Expert from Navigator by double-clicking on the **<Untitled form>** while viewing the forms in a Catalog. During the Form Expert process, associate this form to the **Tools1** table you created earlier. Then select both fields—**APP** and **PATH**—to be included in the form. See Figure 6.4.

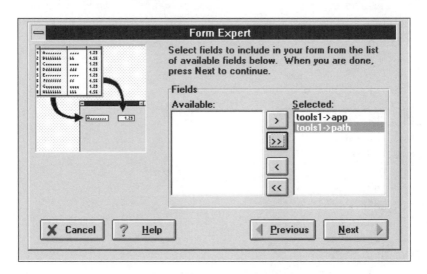

Figure 6.4 During the Form Expert process,
select both fields of Tools1 for use.

If you choose **Browse** layout, Form Expert creates the following object-oriented code:

```
** END HEADER — do not remove this line*
*
LOCAL f
f = NEW DEFAULTFORM()
f.Open()
CLASS DEFAULTFORM OF FORM
   Set Procedure To C:\DBASEWIN\SAMPLES\BUTTONS.CC additive
   this.Height =          20
   this.Text = "Form"
   this.Left =             1
   this.Top =            0
   this.Width =          60
   this.ColorNormal = "N/GB"
   this.HelpId = ""
   this.HelpFile = ""
   this.View = "tools1.dbf"
   DEFINE TEXT TEXT1 OF THIS;
        PROPERTY;
         Height          2.0293,;
         Text "Tools1",;
         Left          1,;
         Top          0.5,;
         Width          18,;
         ColorNormal "RG+/GB",;
         Border .F.,;
         FontSize          18
   DEFINE BROWSE BROWSE1 OF THIS;
        PROPERTY;
         Fields "tools1->:app:,tools1->:path:",;
         Height          15,;
         Left          1,;
         Top          3,;
         Width          50,;
         ColorNormal "N/W",;
         Alias "tools1",;
         FontBold .F.
ENDCLASS
```

After you save the form, use the **Catalog/Edit as Program** menu item to edit the form as code. When the editor window opens, you'll see the code generated by Form Expert.

Modify that code to include the **Browse1.prg** file:

```
#include "browser1.prg"
```

Delete the textbox (**Text1**) definition (you don't need it).

Then redefine the instance of the `Browse` control to use the BR class you defined in **browse1.prg** as follows:

```
DEFINE BR BROWSE1 OF THIS;
    PROPERTY;
        OnLeftDblClick CLASS::BROWSE1_ONLEFTDBLCLICK,;
        Fields "tools1->:app:,tools1->:path:",;
        Height        15.2344,;
        Left          0,;
        Top           0,;
        Width         38.333,;
        ColorNormal "N/W",;
        Alias "tools1",;
        FontBold .F.
```

This code modifies several properties. In addition, this code overrides the `Browse` control's `OnLeftDblClick` event procedure.

The new `OnLeftDblClick` event procedure uses the dBASE for Windows `GetFile` command to allow a user to open a file dialog box to obtain the path of an external code. If the user selects a file (`Len(File1)` > 0), replace the current record's Path field with the path returned by `GetFile`:

```
Procedure BROWSE1_OnLeftDblClick(flags, col, row)
        SET FULLPATH ON
        File1 = GetFile("*.exe")
        If Len(File1) > 0
            Replace Tools1->Path With File1
        EndIf
```

Add this procedure to make life easier for the user. Instead of having to spell out (correctly) the file path, this procedure lets the user select the file (and path) from a file dialog box.

Listing 6.1 shows the complete code for **LAUNSET.WFM**.

Listing 6.1—LAUNSET.WFM

```
** END HEADER — do not remove this line*
*
LOCAL f
f = NEW LAUNSETFORM()
f.Open()


#include "browse1.prg"
CLASS LAUNSETFORM OF FORM
    Set Procedure To C:\DBASEWIN\SAMPLES\BUTTONS.CC additive
    this.OnLeftDblClick = CLASS::FORM_ONLEFTDBLCLICK
    this.HelpId = ""
    this.HelpFile = ""
    this.Text = "Launch Setup"
    this.Height =          15.2344
    this.Left =         0
    this.Top =          0
    this.Width =          38.333
    this.ColorNormal = "N/GB"
    this.View = "tools1.dbf"
    DEFINE BR BROWSE1 OF THIS;
        PROPERTY;
        OnLeftDblClick CLASS::BROWSE1_ONLEFTDBLCLICK,;
        Fields "tools1->:app:,tools1->:path:",;
        Height          15.2344,;
        Left          0,;
        Top          0,;
        Width          38.333,;
        ColorNormal "N/W",;
        Alias "tools1",;
        FontBold .F.
    Procedure BROWSE1_OnLeftDblClick(flags, col, row)
```

```
        SET FULLPATH ON
        File1 = GetFile("*.exe")
        If Len(File1) > 0
            Replace Tools1->Path With File1
        EndIf
ENDCLASS
```

Step 5: Create and Modify a Launch Tools Form

Follow steps similar to those in the previous section to create a second form, **LAUNRUN.WFM**.

As before, edit the form as a program and redefine an instance of the BR class (our defined control class) as follows:

```
DEFINE BR BROWSE1 OF THIS;
        PROPERTY;
        Append .F.,;
        OnLeftDblClick CLASS::BROWSE1_ONLEFTDBLCLICK,;
        Height          6.2939,;
        Left        0,;
        Top         0,;
        Width       14.5,;
        Fields "tools1->:app:"
```

The key differences between this instance of the BR (the custom Browse class) and the base BR class are:

❏ The Append property is set to false. LAUNRUN launches external tools but does not allow a user to edit the **tools1.dbf** table. This protects the data in the **tools1.dbf** table and simplifies the tools launch form (application).

❏ The Fields property specifies that only the app field be shown. The path field is not shown.

❏ The new `OnLeftDblClick` event procedure uses the dBASE for Windows `Run()` command to allow a user to run an external tool (or Windows application):

```
Procedure BROWSE1_OnLeftDblClick(flags, col, row)
    app1 = Tools1->path
    RESULT=RUN(.t.,APP1)
    RETURN
```

Note that the same event name (`OnLeftDblClick`) instigates different behavior in this instance of the `Browse` control than it did in the previous instance. This is an example of polymorphism because the same method (or procedure) name leads to different behavior depending on how each instance of a class defines it.

Note also that in these two example applications each form defines (and *contains*) an instance of the subclass custom `Browse` control (BR). Each time you create an instance of one of these forms, it will automatically contain the new `Browse` control. If you derive new classes of forms based on the LAUNSET or LAUNRUN forms, the new subclasses will also contain a `Browse` control.

Listing 6.2 shows the complete code for **LAUNRUN.WFM**.

Listing 6.2—LAUNRUN.WFM

```
** END HEADER - do not remove this line*
*
LOCAL f
f = NEW LAUNRUNFORM()
f.Open()
#include "browse1.prg"
CLASS LAUNRUNFORM OF FORM
    Set Procedure To C:\DBASEWIN\SAMPLES\BUTTONS.CC additive
    this.HelpId = ""
    this.HelpFile = ""
    this.Text = "Launch Tools1"
    this.Height =          6.2939
    this.Left =          0
    this.Top =          0
```

```
this.Width =           14.5
this.View = "tools1.dbf"
DEFINE BR BROWSE1 OF THIS;
    PROPERTY;
       Append .F.,;
       OnLeftDblClick CLASS::BROWSE1_ONLEFTDBLCLICK,;
       Height           6.2939,;
       Left          0,;
       Top           0,;
       Width           14.5,;
       Fields "tools1->:app:"


  Procedure BROWSE1_OnLeftDblClick(flags, col, row)
       app1 = Tools1->path
       RESULT=RUN(.t.,APP1)
       RETURN
ENDCLASS
```

Figure 6.5 shows LAUNSET during run time.

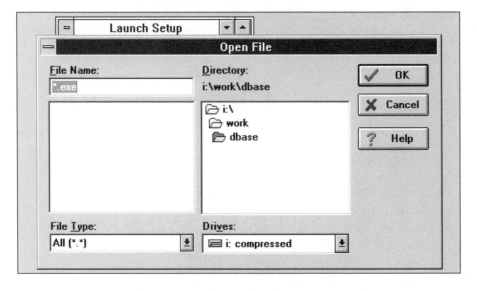

Figure 6.5 LAUNSET during run time.

Figure 6.6 shows LAUNRUN during run time.

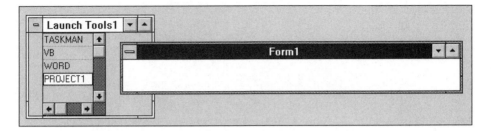

Figure 6.6 LAUNRUN during run time.

dBASE Sum Up

The previous two application examples demonstrate the powerful object-oriented capability of dBASE for Windows. If you're a C++ programmer, you'll have little trouble creating object-oriented dBASE applications. If you're a database programmer from anywhere else, you'll be impressed.

dBASE for Windows is a flexible database development environment, certainly a worthy successor in the dBASE clan. dBASE for Windows is flexible because you don't have to create object-oriented applications as demonstrated in this chapter. Take or leave as much of the object-oriented technology as you want or need.

OOP, Visual Basic Style

Microsoft has taken a somewhat different approach to object-oriented development in Visual Basic 4.0, the 1995 version of this excellent programming system. Although object-oriented, Visual Basic 4.0 has limited OOP capability.

You can define a class in Visual Basic simply by creating a class module from the Visual Basic main menu. Each class module contains one class, and a class module has three properties:

❑ `Creatable`, which determines whether you can use the module to create instances (objects) of this class type

❑ `Name`, the name of the class

❑ `Public`, which determines whether a class is accessible outside the current project

You use the name of the class (designated by the class property) with the keyword `New` to create instances (objects) of the class:

```
Dim NewObject As New ThisClass
```

Each `Sub` or `Function` procedure declared within the class module is the method for the class. Each module-level variable or property (declared using the keyword `Property`) is the class's property. This approach is simple and direct.

Visual Basic, however, is limited in that you cannot create hierarchies of classes. The class stops here. So you can create classes and objects based on these classes that have their own modifications, but you cannot derive new classes from the classes you create. For robust OOP development this is a serious limitation.

To give you a taste for how easy it is to create classes and objects in Visual Basic, the next example creates a database class and then creates an instance (object) of this class from a form.

First, create a new class module using the Visual Basic main menu.

The database class (db1) will contain two tables called **Contact** and **Addresses**. Here's the code to create the contacts table. Add it to the class module. Each `Sub` procedure in the class module is automatically a method for the class. In Visual Basic:

```
Sub CreateContactTable(D As Database)
    Dim Td As New TableDef, Fld() As New Field
    Dim Idx() As New Index, I As Integer
    ReDim Fld(1 To 5), Idx(1 To 2)
    Td.Name = "Contact1"  ' Set the table name.
    ' Create Fields.
    For I = 1 To 4  ' Set properties for fields.
```

```
        Fld(I).Name = Choose(I, "PNum", "LName", "FName",
"Phone")
        Fld(I).Type = Choose(I, DB_LONG, DB_TEXT, DB_TEXT,
DB_TEXT)
        Fld(I).Size = Choose(I, 4, 30, 30, 15)
    Next I
    Fld(1).Attributes = DB_AUTOINCRFIELD    ' Counter field.
    For I = 1 To 4
        Td.Fields.Append Fld(I)
    Next I
    ' Create Table.
    D.TableDefs.Append Td
End Sub
```

Here's the code to create the addresses table. In Visual Basic:

```
Sub CreateAddressTable(D As Database)
    Dim Td As New TableDef, Fld() As New Field
    Dim Idx() As New Index, I As Integer
    ReDim Fld(1 To 5), Idx(1 To 2)
    Td.Name = "Addresses"    ' Set the table name.
    ' Create Fields.
    Fld(1).Attributes = DB_AUTOINCRFIELD    ' Counter field.
    For I = 1 To 5  ' Set properties for fields.
        Fld(I).Name = Choose(I, "ANum", "Addr1", "Addr2",
"CityState", "ZIP")
        Fld(I).Type = Choose(I, DB_LONG, DB_TEXT, DB_TEXT,
DB_TEXT, DB_TEXT)
        Fld(I).Size = Choose(I, 4, 30, 30, 30, 10)
        Td.Fields.Append Fld(I)
    Next I
    ' Create Indexes.
    Idx(1).Name = "PrimaryKey"
    Idx(1).Fields = "ANum"
    Idx(1).Primary = True
    Idx(1).Unique = True
    Idx(2).Name = "City"
```

```
    Idx(2).Fields = "CityState"
    For I = 1 To 2
        Td.Indexes.Append Idx(I)
    Next I
    ' Create Table.
    D.TableDefs.Append Td
End Sub
```

Here's the code to create the new database. In Visual Basic:

```
Sub CreateNewDB()
    Dim Db1 As Database, Dbname As String
    Dbname = "data1.MDB"
    On Error GoTo DBCreateErr
    Set Db1 = CreateDatabase(Dbname, DB_LANG_GENERAL)
    CreateContactTable Db1
    CreateAddressTable Db1
    MsgBox "The database, " & UCase(Dbname) & ", is ready."
    Exit Sub
DBCreateErr:
    Resume Next
End Sub
```

Next, create a form and add a command button to the form. Add the following code to the command button's click event procedure. In Visual Basic:

```
Private Sub Command1_Click()
    Dim Dtabase As New Db1
    Dtabase.CreateNewDB
End Sub
```

This code creates an instance of the database class, db1; then it sends a message to its CreateNewDB method.

Figure 6.7 shows this project in design mode. Listing 6.3 shows the complete code.

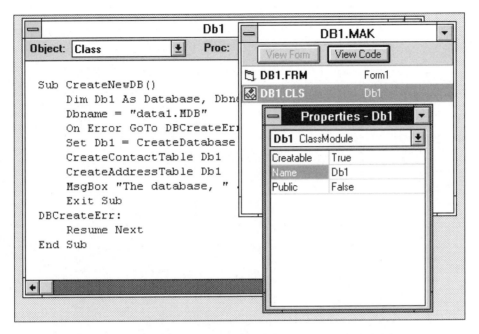

Figure 6.7 **A Visual Basic OOP project in design mode.**

Listing 6.3 **Visual Basic Class Example,** db1

```
' db1.frm
Private Sub Command1_Click()
    Dim Dtabase As New Db1
    Dtabase.CreateNewDB
End Sub
' db1.cls
' class definition of db1 in this class module
' name property has been set to db1
' any code creating an instance (object)
' of this class will declare a New Db1
Sub CreateAddressTable(D As Database)
    Dim Td As New TableDef, Fld() As New Field
    Dim Idx() As New Index, I As Integer
    ReDim Fld(1 To 5), Idx(1 To 2)
```

```
    Td.Name = "Addresses"    ' Set the table name.
    ' Create Fields.
    Fld(1).Attributes = DB_AUTOINCRFIELD    ' Counter field.
    For I = 1 To 5  ' Set properties for fields.
        Fld(I).Name = Choose(I, "ANum", "Addr1", "Addr2",
"CityState", "ZIP")
        Fld(I).Type = Choose(I, DB_LONG, DB_TEXT, DB_TEXT,
DB_TEXT, DB_TEXT)
        Fld(I).Size = Choose(I, 4, 30, 30, 30, 10)
        Td.Fields.Append Fld(I)
    Next I
    ' Create Indexes.
    Idx(1).Name = "PrimaryKey"
    Idx(1).Fields = "ANum"
    Idx(1).Primary = True
    Idx(1).Unique = True
    Idx(2).Name = "City"
    Idx(2).Fields = "CityState"
    For I = 1 To 2
        Td.Indexes.Append Idx(I)
    Next I
    ' Create Table.
    D.TableDefs.Append Td
End Sub
Sub CreateContactTable(D As Database)
    Dim Td As New TableDef, Fld() As New Field
    Dim Idx() As New Index, I As Integer
    ReDim Fld(1 To 5), Idx(1 To 2)
    Td.Name = "Contact1"  ' Set the table name.
    ' Create Fields.
    For I = 1 To 4  ' Set properties for fields.
        Fld(I).Name = Choose(I, "PNum", "LName", "FName",
"Phone")
        Fld(I).Type = Choose(I, DB_LONG, DB_TEXT, DB_TEXT,
DB_TEXT)
        Fld(I).Size = Choose(I, 4, 30, 30, 15)
    Next I
    Fld(1).Attributes = DB_AUTOINCRFIELD    ' Counter field.
```

```
    For I = 1 To 4
        Td.Fields.Append Fld(I)
    Next I
    ' Create Table.
    D.TableDefs.Append Td
End Sub
Sub CreateNewDB()
    Dim Db1 As Database, Dbname As String
    Dbname = "data1.MDB"
    On Error GoTo DBCreateErr
    Set Db1 = CreateDatabase(Dbname, DB_LANG_GENERAL)
    CreateContactTable Db1
    CreateAddressTable Db1
    MsgBox "The database, " & UCase(Dbname) & ", is ready."
    Exit Sub
DBCreateErr:
    Resume Next
End Sub
```

Wrap-Up

This wraps up our specific discusssions of the OOP implementations you've explored in this book. As you can see, the path is varied. Your needs must determine which of these (or other) OOP implementations you use. If you want all the control you can get in a programming environment and language, then C++ might be your best bet.

If you're a higher-level developer, then Delphi, dBASE for Windows, and Visual Basic offer powerful, differing OOP views. I think choosing among these systems is more or less a matter of taste and style. OOP remains truly within the spirit of the Tao.

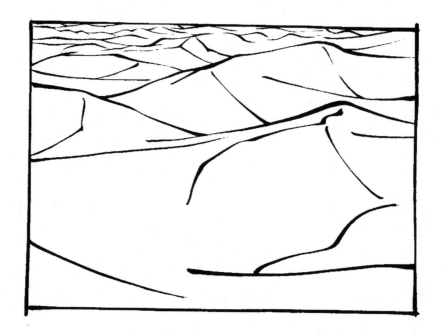

Chapter Seven

Designing with Objects

If you want to shrink something, you must first allow it to expand. If you want to take something, you must first allow it to be given. This is called the subtle perception of the way things are.

—Lao-tzu

Any program when running is obsolete. If a program is useful, it will have to be changed. Any program will expand to fill all memory.

—Utz's Law

> *Not even our technological evolution has been a linear move-*
> *ment from lower to higher levels, but rather a process punctu-*
> *ated by massive regressions.*

> —Riane Eisler

The way of objects described in this book is a process for designing programs that evolve in step with the world they model. Programs composed
of objects are more powerful and flexible because of their built-in capacity
for change. In this chapter, we'll reshape the object-oriented techniques
we've discussed so far into a design philosophy.

Structured design suggests that you stop, think, and work out all the
details before you start coding. Because most programmers use some form
of structured design, you may expect an object-oriented design philosophy
to be another complicated methodology requiring a long learning curve,
excessive self-discipline, numerous diagrams and rules, and reams of documentation. It doesn't necessarily involve any of those, but it does require
a fresh perspective.

Let's back up a little and briefly review structured design to see the
kinds of problems software engineers must consider.

An Alternative to Chaos

Programmers often use guidelines to determine the best way to design a
program. A *methodology* is a set of guidelines applied sequentially to generate a design from a set of specifications. Methodologies are popular
because they give a step-by-step process for getting from the problem to
the solution.

Structured programming was the first alternative to the lack of structure that led to chaos in large programming projects. This style emphasizes the structuring of programs into a pyramid shape like that found in
the traditional business organizational chart. The bottom of the pyramid
represents the blue-collar workers, the managers are at the top, and the
middle contains the go-betweens who receive general commands from the
managers and interpret them into specific commands for the workers.

A structured methodology generates a well-documented system into a model that's relatively easy to understand. It takes a system specification (a description of what the system should do) and generates a structured design. The methodology we'll examine here was pioneered by Yourdon, Constantine, and DeMarco and has been extended by Ward and Mellor to include real-time and data-driven systems.

You begin by describing the system (using the system specification, which was generated from the system analysis) with a series of data-flow diagrams. A DFD is a collection of bubbles and arrows. Each bubble represents a process or transformation that accepts data (incoming arrows) and produces a new type of data (outgoing arrows). Figure 7.1 shows a single bubble.

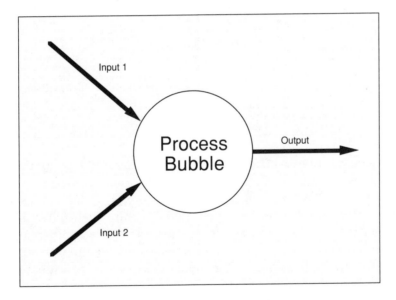

Figure 7.1 **Each bubble in a DFD represents a process or transformation.**

An entire system or a subset of a system can be represented by a single bubble. The process of arranging a system into a hierarchy of DFDs is called *leveling* (because the system is partitioned into levels of complexity). The DFD modeling process leads to a complete set of diagrams representing the system at various levels of complexity.

Bubbles let you view the system from different perspectives, from overview (a single diagram with one bubble and little detail) to fine detail (many diagrams, each with multiple bubbles).

Once you've generated and checked the detailed DFDs, you generate a hierarchical structure chart from them (Figure 7.2). You can think of it as the business organization chart for the program.

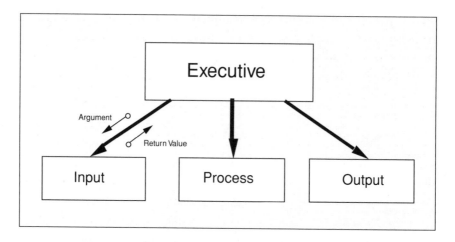

Figure 7.2 Hierarchical structure chart generated from DFDs.

The chart shows data moving in and out of boxes, which represent the transformations. It also shows which modules call which other modules. Combined with information about the data structures and transformations, the chart lets you code the program's components one at a time independently of other components. Each box represents a function, and the data moving in and out of the box represent function arguments and return values.

What's Wrong with This Picture?

Structured techniques generate a much more maintainable design than anything produced with earlier techniques. So what's wrong with them? For starters—complexity, exhaustive design, and excessive documentation. But what can we do to improve them?

The high cost of software maintenance prompted the development of structured techniques, which are actually a way to generate good documentation for a system. Good documentation, of course, allows follow-up programmers to grasp what's going on, fix problems quickly, and expand the system. It also lowers maintenance costs, to a point. The system's design may be clear but as restrictive as if the programmers had simply started coding.

How can we take a popular structured technique and apply it to object-oriented design? A DFD assumes that a data element just flows around the system and passes through bubbles, where it's processed. DFDs stem from the perspective that all memory is a public resource. In this model, data elements are passive, raw materials that are acted upon by little processing plants (functional modules).

In an object-oriented design, messages move around the system, but "flow" isn't a particularly useful way of thinking about their movement. Objects keep their data to themselves and perform operations on their own data, eliminating the potential for the wrong functions acting on the right data and vice versa.

If you think of objects as little programs (or task-specific applications), the only useful place for DFDs is inside the object itself, and that's not very satisfying or helpful. DFDs are inappropriate for object-oriented design (ditto for structure charts) for at least one good reason—they don't provide the kind of information you need. You should approach with a healthy dose of skepticism any object-oriented methodology that purports to use them.

(Beware of methodologies that use the input-processing-output scheme to develop the system model, as in, "The input to the transmogrification phase is the annotated, fully redacted Framis Phase Model. The output is a Smith Perfection Chart showing all the completely specified objects and their interrelationships." This sort of thinking is part of the evolution from structured to object-oriented design. Expect to find it in early methodologies. When the first steam engine was installed on a boat, the designers attempted to take the rotary power from the steam engine and make it pull a set of oars, pick them up out of the water, move them forward, put them in the water, and so on. They didn't realize that a leap into a new methodology was necessary.)

In addition, the requirement (imposed by procedural languages) that all problems be massaged until they resemble computers leads to static designs and further problems. In other words, we try to make the problem conform to the computer and not vice versa. Although the implementation might be well documented, a design change usually requires that we return to the beginning of the series of transformations that generated the design. Only at the beginning does the representation of the system map directly to the problem in the world.

In other words, the design isn't an accurate representation of the real-world system we're attempting to model. Instead, it represents the solution we build in the computer. Thus, it doesn't change easily when the real-world situation changes or our understanding of the problem changes.

Because a program inevitably changes and because programmers (and managers) don't want to spend the time required to document those changes, the program's maintainers begin to encroach upon the original boundaries of the design. Eventually, these boundaries become fuzzy and the clarity of the design is lost—all because the design process requires too many transformations and too much documentation to support easy changes. In the words of guru Larry Fogg, "Too much magic causes software rot."

In most traditional organizations, change is an enemy or, at best, a mysterious entity to be avoided. Consider the plight of many traditional businesses faced with changing markets. In the past, changes could be slowly integrated into the company after months or years of consideration. Now, things are happening too quickly for every change to be propagated all the way to the top of the organization, learned by the CEO and the board of directors before it's implemented, and propagated back down.

Management consultants are proposing that individual workers be given the power and responsibility to make the adaptations that affect their work. Those who are directly affected by something should be able to experiment with it. They see the changes first, can see how a system should evolve, and are the first to notice the effects of any adaptations. They're in the best position to experiment. In theory, they make the best decisions.

Programmers, too, must be in a position to experiment for both creative and practical reasons. Object-oriented design encourages such experimentation.

If you're using structured design techniques now, you should continue to use them with object-oriented programming. Just remember that older structured design techniques don't support inheritance or formal reuse, whereas these notions are of primary concern when you're designing object-oriented systems. You must apply a bit of careful judgment and ad hoc techniques to solve these problems.

Real-time structured design methods (such as Ward-Mellor) and entity-relationship diagrams are good starting points for object-oriented design. Object-oriented programming builds on structured programming; if you're using good structured techniques, you should build on what works but design with a bit more flexibility to accommodate reuse.

Programming for Change

Consider how you interact with the world. You begin by collecting the best information you can and creating a model of the world based on that information. (This happens, of course, at brainwave speed.) Then you behave based on that model.

The model is inevitably flawed, and every moment of your life you gain new experience and have new thoughts that modify your model of the world. You conceive multiple models to represent various aspects of the world. Many of these models are regularly updated (by new technology, new programming techniques, how you perceive a compiler's operation, the ways you communicate), whereas others may continue to work just fine for your purposes and don't need to be updated (the nocturnal activities of the African dung beetle, the latest improvements to Basic). You constantly modify your models to adapt to new external and internal information.

As you use a model of the world, you almost always gain new information from it and change the model accordingly. In fact, if a model stops changing, chances are that you aren't using it. In a sense, the model is a state indicator of the learning process.

Suppose you move to a new area and need to go to the grocery store. You get a map and study it until you discover a way to get there. On the way, you observe your surroundings and remember them, making a model in your head. The model encompasses only a portion of the area you live in, but if it gets you to the grocery store it's extremely functional. As you go new places, you expand your model of the area until you can get to many places without consulting a map.

Let's look at the same example using structured techniques, which require all the research up front. You would have to memorize the entire map before you went anywhere. What if the map changes or the streets don't correspond to the map? There isn't much allowance for change unless you redraw portions of the map and memorize it again. We don't know anyone who works this way, but programmers are expected to.

Suppose you wanted to take up photography. Books on photography are plentiful, and you could read indefinitely about how to take pictures, but at some point you'd need to get out and take some pictures yourself to relate to the text you're reading.

The model we create when we build a computer program is similar to the one we create when we represent something from the outside world within ourselves. The computer expression of the model is more concrete, is in a different medium, and takes longer to change, but it still expresses our current understanding of an external system. In the same way that we change our models of the world to adapt to new internal or external information, we want to change our computer models of the world to adapt to exactly the same kind of information. Why not behave as if design were a learning process?

Here are four object-oriented design guidelines:

1. Keep in mind that you can't know everything about a system before you design it. Don't even try. Some things can be learned only when the system is running for the first time (or when it's been running for a week or a year).

2. Your goal should be to get something working as soon as possible and to use the model to gain further information about the problem.

   Your first model may be only vaguely like the external system (remember how you thought cars worked when you were in kindergarten?), but the ideas can be refined and modified as you learn. Object-oriented programming supports change, so use that to your advantage. It also prevents "overkill programming"—spending too much time creating a program to solve problems that will never arise.

   Use creeping featurism but add the features as they're requested to allow immediate feedback. Object-oriented programming tends to isolate the effects of one part of a system from another, so changing one part of a model usually doesn't affect other parts.

3. Plan on changing the design as you go. This doesn't mean "Do something and throw it away," as previous techniques have suggested, but rather "Start someplace reasonable and grow as you learn." The goal is not to create a static design, so assume from the start that the design will change.

4. It's OK to make mistakes, but try to make them as early in the process as you can. The best way to find out whether you've made a mistake is to try out your design. Your mistake is probably isolated, so you won't throw the entire design away; instead, you'll just modify a section to reflect your new learning.

One of the old bugaboos of structured programming and design is management's desire to measure programmer productivity. Object-oriented programming and design increase productivity by providing libraries of objects that can be reused and by allowing the production of more generic, easier-to-maintain code.

Unfortunately, it's hard to measure the effect that object-oriented programming has on programmer productivity. Most of the standard metrics are based on measuring lines of code written. With object-oriented programming, we want to measure lines of code *not* written: the amount of code reused across other applications. We don't have tools that do this today, but perhaps future browsers and inspectors will keep track of when we reuse code. For programmer productivity to increase, reuse must be rewarded.

Object-Oriented System Design

It would be convenient—but, unfortunately, unrealistic—to expect programmers and users to have complete knowledge of the system. First, we can seldom delude ourselves into believing that we know the system at any given time; second, the system we're designing and the techniques (the compilers, languages, and hardware) we're using are evolving. Most of us approximate and speculate at every turn.

On the less technical, more personal side, two convenient approximations are often made in software design projects: The designer completely understands the problem before beginning, and the user reads the manual and thus knows the program completely before using it.

Demanding perfection from users simply isn't practical. Many system designers acknowledge that users probably don't read the manual and may at first understand only a fraction of what the program is supposed to do. These enlightened designers make the system work for the user by anticipating that users will be diverse and evolving. The system must allow users to learn (modify their internal models) and to adapt the system when their problems change (adapt to external changes).

Object-oriented design offers a solution: You can design objects at any time, whenever the need moves you. Every system is assumed to be in flux; every program is assumed to be dynamic. You can create, modify, and delete new objects at run time without disrupting the system.

Say you're designing an editor. You began (sensibly enough) by creating a `file_editor` type. This type can open a file, read it into a buffer, move a cursor around in the buffer, find text, insert and delete text, and so on. As the type definition develops, so does the need to test it. You decide that the simplest way to do that is to make the type aware of the screen. In other words, the type will show you on the screen what it's doing off-screen.

To be aware, the `file_editor` screen must have some knowledge of how text can be displayed. It needs to know where the display starts and ends and where the cursor should sit on the screen—in short, how to map the buffer to the screen. You add these features and everything works. Now you begin testing the `file_editor` features, one by one.

Two things happen. First, by using the system in a screen editor, you begin to see possibilities you hadn't before imagined. Because the text display can vary and can be controlled, you realize that multiple pieces of text can exist on the screen at one time. Second, you now want to use the `file_editor` to display everything—multiple files, sections of text for prompting, help screens, even the line at the bottom of the editor that prompts for input for text searches and other activities. Thus, the `file_editor` type is undergoing a reuse test.

Does the type adapt itself easily to these new situations? After answering "no," you begin modifying the type to make it more general and soon run afoul of the complexity test.

With all the files, views, and cursors, one change can create many new problems. The file_editor type is failing the overambitious-object test: It tries to do too much and as a result can't be reused. A mature type, especially one that has evolved through several redesigns, often becomes too complex for further evolution. Take confusing complexity as a sign that an object has a design problem. It may not, but it's worth a look.

In this case, you discover a better design when reusing the file_editor. You should have created a text_buffer type that knows about big chunks of text, how to move around in the text, how to insert and delete, and so on. This type can be used for files, constant strings, standard input, and one-line user prompts with equal ease.You then derive from type text_buffer a file_buffer that knows how to read and write files (write() is a virtual function in text_buffer). Finally, a text_viewer type contains a text_buffer, either a plain one or a file_buffer (because virtual functions are used, it doesn't need to know the specifics).

A text_viewer knows all about views of the text—starting and ending points of the piece being displayed, the display cursor, and so on. It resolves the changes in a text_buffer with the way it appears onscreen. (It also isolates the changes necessary when going to a new platform or changing from text-mode to graphics-mode displays.)

The need to design, experiment, and create occurs every time you (the designer) interact with the system. It isn't isolated in any of the activities (object discovery, object assembly, system construction, system maintenance, and object reuse) because you're always learning new things about the internal and external factors and about design itself.

Only in the simplest cases will you understand the entire problem and get the design correct the first time. It's a koan: To design it you have to build it, but to build it you have to design it. In the end, the system grows, so it's important to germinate as soon as possible. Start building, and you'll start designing.

The Five Stages of Object Design

Let's look at a way to tackle object-oriented programming. I've used this approach successfully and have observed that programmers' attention is held during the design process because they can immediately apply the design or imagine how it will work in code. This design approach, like object-oriented programming itself, thrives on being as close as possible to the end result.

This technique assumes that type design is driven by system design (you can't develop good types in a vacuum), that a type doesn't spring fully formed and perfect from the head of its creator, and that a type is mature only after it has been modified a few times to meet the creator's changing external needs and internal understanding.

Throughout this discussion, remember that the only goal is to define the object types. If you see a better approach to your problem, try it! What counts is coming up with a good set of types. The test of your design will be how well it models the situation in the real world and not whether you followed the proper steps in producing it.

You may think that it takes years of experience to design types properly and to know to put a particular function member or data in a type. To dispel this myth and prevent you from wasting time on early design decisions, let's look at this five-step technique for describing the creation and maturation of types.

1. **Object discovery:** This is when you try to determine which object types will solve the problems your system presents. At this point, you're more concerned with the boundaries and gross interactions between objects than with the details. We'll take a closer look at this step shortly.

2. **Object assembly:** As you start building the objects, you'll discover that you need data and function members to make the internals of the objects work properly. You may also discover that you need other objects, either as members of the type or to work in concert with an object in the system. A good way to uncover further type requirements during object assembly is to develop and test programs for each type you create.

3. **System construction:** As you bring objects together in the final program, the system may require either new functionality in existing objects or entirely new objects.

4. **System extension:** In object-oriented programming, the dreaded system maintenance becomes just another step in the process. And it's not unpleasant—it's exciting because making a well-designed system more powerful is so easy. This is where you'll discover how well your system is designed. If it isn't as easy to extend as you'd like, expect to find weak points in your design. Once you find them, you can fix them.

   Note that activities focus on object types, not systems. *Maintenance* means maintaining object types, the discrete subparts of your system. If your object types are "clean," building and modifying the system is simple.

5. **Object reuse:** When you build a new program using old object types, your new needs will stress the types' design. If the design doesn't easily fit into a new situation, here's where it will show up, and you'll see the parts that need to be changed.

At each stage, you get new information to guide you in type design. Although it would be difficult and time-consuming to anticipate this information in a preemptive design, the information comes to you naturally as you pass through these stages. Although this philosophy of object-oriented design differs from past methodologies, implementing it is easy. In fact, many programmers tend to work this way regardless of the methodology they're supposed to be following.

More on Object Discovery

The first of the five stages merits a closer look. What criteria do you use to discover objects? Here are some guidelines:

❑ Look for external factors, those necessary for interactions between objects and the world outside the system. You may discover some data members and methods at this point, but you'll primarily be discovering the objects themselves.

❏ Look for boundaries in the real world. For example, the boundary between memory and disk is often reflected as a boundary in your system.

❏ Look for things that are duplicated in a system. In a keyboard, for instance, `button` is an obvious object. A car has four wheels and four doors; an air traffic control system deals with planes. If you add new types of planes to the air traffic control system, for example, it should still know how to handle them.

❏ Hunt for the least common denominator in a system (the smallest unit). If you're manipulating text, that could be a character, a word, a line, or a group of text with the same attributes, depending on how you intend to use the text.

❏ Think of new situations in which you might use the type. Does it work? Does it adapt easily? Imagine, for example, a very large version of your system or your system in a new situation with new requirements or constraints.

❏ Separate the actions and characteristics (or properties) that change from those that stay the same.

❏ List the data your system needs to know about. Look for data that seem to belong together. Collect these data elements into an object.

❏ Look for data you want to hide or protect from careless modification. Such things usually belong inside an object.

❏ Look for common interfaces between objects and put them into an abstract base type.

❏ Imagine the types you'd need to put the project together right now. To find out the kind of functionality they need, write `main()` as if you had those types.

❏ Look for initialization and cleanup activities. These should be performed inside constructors and destructors.

An Example

Consider a sophisticated management system that attempts to solve the problems inherent in setting up a video store. Most such stores are an exercise in frustration: You know the kinds of movies you want, but you usually don't know the titles you want.

By reading the box containing the video, you see what the movie distributor wants you to see ("This movie is *Star Wars, Lawrence of Arabia, Rancho Deluxe,* and *Gone with the Wind* all rolled into one. Every single reviewer loved it!"). You also get a three-paragraph description of the movie, written by someone who may or may not have viewed it and who was in any case bound to say positive things. You won't find valuable information. For instance, if all the movie reviewers gave it a thumbs-down, no reviewers will be quoted on the box. It won't tell you whether all your neighbors hated it or the amount of humor, sex, or violence in the movie. These are things you can find out only by renting the movie.

Now imagine a video store that doesn't have shelves filled with movie cartons. Instead, you step up to a computer (or to a person operating a computer) and say, "Today I'm in the mood for a movie with a science-fiction theme that's set in the near future, that my favorite reviewers liked, and that has moderate levels of nudity and low levels of profanity and violence."

The machine then brings up the titles of movies you haven't seen and that aren't currently checked out and puts them in order according to your personal profile. You can get more information about each title, such as the actors and directors, reviews, biographies of the people involved in making the movie, and even a graphical picture of the box (if you insist). If the movie was never released in theaters and thus was not reviewed, you can get other criteria, such as the results of a poll of people who have viewed the movie (including information about gender and age group). In short, you get the kind of information you really need to select a movie.

When you choose a movie, the clerk gets it from the back and uses a bar-code reader to enter the number into the computer, which generates a receipt and does all the necessary bookkeeping.

Part of this video-store management system is obviously an elaborate database system (which needs to be updated easily at regular intervals and from various sources, including the customers themselves). Part of it is the user interface, part is the bar-code interface, and part is the bookkeeping system.

The Object-Oriented Design System

To set up object discovery, make lists of:

❏ Data (information that the system needs to know or remember).

❏ Events (situations the system needs to respond to).

❏ Functionality (what the system needs to do).

❏ Obvious objects (anything that leaps out at you). For example, you may know from the beginning that you want to use a windowing interface.

Don't try to make these lists perfect or complete—the act of putting together the model (not creating a list) will ensure that the system is complete. The lists only act as ticklers to help you find the objects in your system. By looking at the lists, you'll see patterns that suggest objects. When you discover enough objects to describe the system without the lists, you'll throw the lists away.

For some systems, the data list will give you the most information and will be the easiest to compile. Other systems will be primarily event-driven (usually referred to as *real-time* systems); for others, you may think more easily in terms of what you want it to do, so the functionality list will be the easiest.

Remember that it's OK to make mistakes or omit things—an object-oriented system makes it easy to modify the program when you discover inconsistencies with the real world. Because objects keep their data and functions to themselves, changes in the system tend to be localized rather than propagated throughout the system (as in procedural languages).

When you compile the data list, feel free to group data items that are likely to form an object. For example, a `person` object will probably contain a name, address, age, sex, membership number, and list of movies the person has seen, so it makes sense to combine those items.

Events aren't always as obvious as data. A mouse, for instance, is actually an event generator. Every time you push a button or the mouse crosses a boundary, that's an event. We usually handle events by creating a representation of a state and changing that state based on the current state and the current event. We often refer to this as a *state machine*. The rest of the system makes decisions based on the current state.

For example, we can implement a context-sensitive help system with a state machine. Every time the user changes context (by making a selection from a menu, for example), the help state machine changes state. When the user asks for help, the type of help given depends on the state (the context). Looking at a collection of events will often help you discover an object.

(It's interesting to think of the current moment as an external factor while it's happening but as an internal factor as soon as it's past. It changes the state of the individual. We can think of the individual as a state machine that changes based on input from external factors.)

Keep in mind that this is an iterative process, an approach intended only to give you a framework and get you started. The framework may change as you sketch out the system, but in the end it's unimportant—the goal is to determine what your objects should be. As you fill in the details of your sketch, you'll discover new objects and new relationships between objects.

Let's begin by compiling the four lists for our video-store management system:

DATA

Customer
    Name
    Address
    Customer ID
    List of movies previously checked out
    Preference list
    Profile
Movie
    Name
    Quantity
    Price Structure
    Evaluation List
Rental Transaction
    Date
    Customer
    Movie list (What if not all movies are returned?)
Business report
    Date range
    Data list
    Data format
    Calculations

EVENTS

Customer asks for range of movies.
Customer asks for further data on movie.
    Reviews
    Local opinion
    Box description/pictures
    Personnel: actors, directors, and so on
    Theater runs and receipts
Customer checks out movie(s).
Customer asks for computer-generated movie selection based on customer profile.
Customer asks for best-seller based on overall popularity.
Customer returns movies (possibly not all), possibly checks out more.
Customer gives opinion of movie.
New movies arrive.
New movie data arrives.
Old movies are discarded/replaced.
Manager requests report.

FUNCTIONALITY

Create new customer profile.
Create new movie profile.
Create movie request profile; combine with customer profile.
Search for appropriate movies.
Create management report.
Check out movie.
Check in movie.
Update profiles.

OBVIOUS OBJECTS

Windows
Database
Error handler
Time and date string

After putting these lists together, you need to begin discovering objects. By this time, you may already have seen some objects (in the data list, for instance, where a group of data—customer, movie, rental transaction, and business report—obviously belongs together).

Functionality may require more work. You may want to put it in a block chart as shown in Figure 7.3.

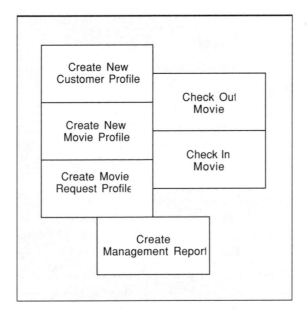

Figure 7.3 **Block diagram.**

Now take an individual section and begin analyzing it for objects. Think about what you want that section to produce. (Will the "thing" produced be an object? Will the producer be an object?) What do you want to be portable, or at least retargetable (the user interface, other hardware, the operating system interface)? Wrap these in an object.

Does the block diagram suggest any boundaries that reveal new objects? In a networking system, for example, the network itself is a boundary; you may need to create "transaction objects" to send across the network.

As you discover objects, consider what those objects need to know. Should they maintain this information themselves or get it from another object? Make a note of that object, even if it belongs in another section.

Notice in the functionality list the recurrence of the word *profile*. This may suggest an abstract concept called *profile* that you represent in an abstract base type. All profiles may then be derived from that type. This is just an early observation, however, and in the end may not be appropriate.

The Complexity Test

Make sure that your objects don't become too complex. Just because you need a particular object, that object need not be part of a single type rather than a type hierarchy or composition. Don't fall victim to "premature specification."

In an earlier example concerning the file-editing type, the type's complexity was revealed during code reuse. The type was difficult to apply to a new situation because it was specific to a certain problem. The solution was to factor it into smaller, more discrete parts.

If you have a background in structured techniques, you may recognize the complexity test as equivalent to testing for low coupling and high cohesion. This is a little harder to judge with objects, because coupling and cohesion have been tests for functions. An object that does what you want always looks great; the test of goodness comes when you try to reuse it.

The complexity test is also important during object assembly, when you'll discover whether your objects are too complex. As you add and test functions, things may get out of hand. Adding new functions will be difficult because the type is managing so much by itself. This is an indication that the type needs to be factored into smaller sections and assembled through inheritance or composition.

Factoring results in several types, each of which is easier to implement because it's easier to think about. In addition, the objects will probably be easier to reuse.

OOP and GUI

One of the areas where object-oriented programming pays off most is in graphical user interfaces, such as Microsoft Windows, OS/2 Presentation Manager, and the Macintosh's operating system. This is due in part to the inherent complexity of programming for GUI systems.

This might seem paradoxical, considering how easy these systems are for application users. If you look under the hood of a GUI application, however, you'll find that everything that's easy for the user requires hard work on the part of the programmer. Windows has an Application Programming Interface of many, many functions that must be called to do things such as create a window, select the font, invalidate areas of the screen, track the mouse, and so on. OS/2 Presentation Manager is even more complex.

Object-oriented programming languages help hide the complexity of GUI programming by providing objects that encapsulate access to the API. After all, you probably want a window in your application that's just like the standard window type, but a little different. With an object-oriented language, you don't need to learn and make dozens of function calls to create a window. Instead, you need only know about the predefined object types and then use inheritance to add new behaviors. With OOP, it's easy to reuse shared resources, such as buttons, boxes, and forms. All Windows applications use the same GUI "pieces."

Another, more subtle reason for the link between GUI systems and object-oriented programming is that most graphical systems are message-based. For example, Windows and OS/2 treat user events (such as clicking the mouse or pressing a key) as messages sent to the application. In the OOP world, you can send these messages directly to the corresponding window object and handle it just like any other method in the system. This means that less code is required to process user events in an object-oriented language.

Libraries and Frameworks

Part of the strength of object-oriented programming lies in the creation of libraries of reusable objects. Many commercial vendors now create libraries for Delphi, C++, dBASE, Visual Basic, and others. These libraries provide generic types for user-interface components such as windows, dialog boxes, and database management tools. Using libraries is a great way to increase your productivity and (usually) to get examples of good object-oriented programming techniques.

If you extend the notion of abstraction one step beyond such visual elements as windows and dialog boxes, you can conceive of generic applications themselves. A library that allows you to extend a generic application is known as an *application framework*. You can think of an application framework as a do-nothing application that can be extended to do almost anything. Although programming with an application framework may seem unfamiliar at first, it builds on many of the concepts presented here to give you an even higher level of productivity.

Skeptic's Corner

You may be saying to yourself, "This makes a lot of sense. It's pretty much the way I write programs anyway. But what about large projects? Will this technique still apply?"

Remember that object-oriented programming supports systems that change throughout their lifetime. The model focuses on the process rather than the goal. Your objective, then, should not be to build a system but to "grow" a system. The most elaborate garden must be planted; the objects in the garden grow at their own rates. At each stage of development, the garden has an effect. It may not be mature, but it's functional.

It's also real—something people can look at, work with, and improve. You can see how things work now and imagine a direction to move in the context of the current system. If some plants aren't effective in the garden, you pull them out and plant something else. Eventually, with time and continuous design, the garden matures into a phase in which change consists of only minor adjustments.

You could design a garden as a finished system and use fully mature plants that look exactly the way you want them. This approach is expensive initially and expensive to change. The fact that you have good plans (good documentation) helps you understand the vision of the original designer, but it doesn't take into consideration that the requirements of the world may change or that you may understand something the original designer didn't. You'll still have to develop new plans for a major change and tear out expensive plants. Even minor changes (those that don't involve design changes) are expensive because a system such as this isn't designed to be modified; it's designed with the assumption that it's finished.

Object-oriented programming lets you start with a small garden and eventually increase the acreage, start with a large garden of immature plants (some of which may be changed as the garden matures), or start with older, existing plants and add young, new ones. Not only can you build programs more quickly, but the programs can also be adapted to the new knowledge and new situations that have been the nemesis of old-style programming techniques.

The Art of Software Design

All this makes object-oriented design sound a lot like art, which isn't a bad analogy. Creating software, like creating art, requires interpretation on the part of the artists; calling it "engineering" may be one of the more creative misapplications of that word. Getting a group of artists to work together is a difficult process; they focus on the product, not the company. There's no physical structure (such as a manufacturing plant) in a software group to hold it together once the project is complete.

Can object-oriented programming techniques change this? Probably. One person can manage much larger, more complex bodies of code. Reuse of libraries of existing code is supported. The compiler controls the integration of a project, so you don't rely on tests that may or may not be created and administered. Objects are little programs, so each person can have the satisfaction of creating a complete work, even if it is later integrated into a larger one. All this helps teams create and work together and improves accountability, localization of bugs and changes, learning in a large project, and flexibility.

Structured techniques came about because existing languages couldn't support large projects—things broke down when the projects got too big, and a great deal of planning was necessary to prevent this breakdown. Using an object-oriented language that supports large projects, you can plan a lot less, code sooner, and test the real thing (or something close to it) instead of trying to imagine whether it will be what you want.

During object assembly, consider the initialization and cleanup of each object. Should these activities be part of object discovery and CASE support? Almost certainly.

You're "growing" your objects from the time you start thinking about them. Writing them is the rapid phase of growth, but growth nonetheless: You start with the type framework and then add and test functions and function bodies. During system construction and extension, you may add more to the type.

Object design occurs in all five stages: object discovery, object assembly, system construction, system extension (not maintenance), and object reuse—throughout the lifetime of a system. We've only pretended we could force design to occur in the first phases of a project, and not later, thinking that this would make it less expensive to maintain. Good documentation helps, but things still change and new designs are still required. A rigid design, no matter how well it's documented, eventually loses its internal structure in the face of these changes.

And that's it for this introductory study of object-oriented techniques. I hope you can see that the sophisticated techniques in object-oriented programming languages help programmers create more productive, creative, flexible programs designed to evolve with the real-world problems they model. Object-oriented programming is both a method and a philosophy, one that can dramatically narrow the gap between the real world and the world of the computer.

Afterword

I've left Zack Urlocker's Afterword from the first edition intact because it casts an illuminating perspective on the development of OOP since 1990.

—Gary Entsminger

Never make predictions, especially about the future.

—Samuel Goldwyn

Samuel Goldwyn may not be an Eastern philosopher, but his words ring true. Despite his advice, I'm going to look ahead at the future of object-oriented programming. But first, you may be wondering how this Afterword came about.

About two-and-a-half years ago, I spoke with Gary about doing an article on object-oriented programming for the now-legendary *Micro Cornucopia*. Strangely enough, I also met Bruce Eckel through the pages of that magazine. His article on C++ appeared a few pages after mine, so it's fitting that the three of us meet again in print in Gary's book on the philosophy and practice of object-oriented programming.

I recently had the pleasure of working with Bruce on Borland's OOP World Tour, where we taught object-oriented programming in C++ and Turbo Pascal around the world. At our final destination, Tokyo, the two of us took a train out to the old capital, Kamakura, and explored the variety of temples there. As we walked through the exquisite gardens, amidst the statues and trees, Bruce told me about Gary's book on the Tao of objects. It sounded like a fascinating way to learn about object-oriented programming. After all, programming is part art, part science, and certainly part philosophy. One of the areas we talked about was the future of object-oriented programming.

The philosophical side of object-oriented programming may well endure beyond structured programming and design as well as other programming approaches. But as you continue down the path of object-oriented programming seeking your own enlightenment, it's sometimes reassuring to know that the art and science are maturing. For this reason, I was asked to look further down the path to see what's in store for object-oriented programmers. Along the way I'll discuss the evolution of hardware and software, the impact on OOP, tools beyond OOP, and some of the myths of object-oriented programming.

The Evolution of Hardware and Software

One of the obvious trends that affects object-oriented programming is the changing hardware. As I look across my desk to the "computer museum" in the corner of my office, I can see the progress hardware has made in the past decade. We've gone from 64K Z80 CP/M machines such as the Osborne I that ran Ron Cain's Small-C and Turbo Pascal 1.0 (and had room to spare!) to my new 4 MB 386SX that runs Turbo C++ and Turbo Pascal 6.0. And I'm not at all surprised by the fact that the Osborne cost more than the 386. Certainly we'll see the same level of improvements in hardware in the next decade. My 386, barely a month old, is already considered old hat by the hardware aficionados touting the latest 486s. Let them laugh; I'll catch up with the 586 or perhaps even the 686.

So what impact does this have on our software? Utz's law, as Gary stated in Chapter 7, tells us that "any program will expand to fill all memory." My current crop of C++ and Turbo Pascal tools doesn't exhaust all my RAM, but by the time I load a few TSRs and Windows 3.0 the ceiling is definitely in sight.

Utz must have been thinking about graphical environments when he coined his law. Much of the hardware horsepower we have achieved in the last 10 years has gone toward making powerful, easy-to-use environments such as Windows. These environments make computing what it should be: easy, powerful, and fun.

But as any programmer knows, the easier you make things for the user, the harder they are for the developer. Programming for today's graphical environments is exceedingly difficult using traditional tools. So if Windows is the future, how do programmers get there? The answer is, of course, by using object-oriented programming.

If you look at the development tools used in graphical environments, you'll see that an overwhelming majority are object-oriented. Certainly DOS programmers benefit from OOP, but in graphical environments it has become a necessity.

In some sense, the rapidly expanding hardware field has forced us down the path of object-oriented programming. And although there's a learning curve to adopting OOP, it's one that's worth overcoming.

The more you use OOP, the more excited you'll become. As one programmer put it, "When I program in OOP, I'm limited only by my imagination." Many programmers find that walls of complexity prevent them from building certain kinds of applications. With OOP, these barriers come tumbling down, slowly at first, then in an avalanche as you learn to create self-contained objects that tackle small problems for you. Your job is to piece these objects together into larger programs that take us into new application areas. After all, we've got to do something with the extra cycles on the 686.

OOP Horizons

Object-oriented technology will continue to improve over the next decade. Already the current crop of OOP tools from Borland, Zortech, The Whitewater Group, and others are in their second or later versions with major enhancements over earlier ones. Efforts toward standardization with groups such as ANSI and the Object Management Group, combined with the competitiveness of the marketplace, will ensure continued improvement in the languages. This means faster compilation, better run-time performance, and better tools for browsing, inspecting, and debugging.

I also expect that we'll continue to have a wide spectrum of OOP languages. The hybrid languages will coexist with pure OOP languages for years to come. And, as has happened in the past, newer languages will build on the OOP concepts that exist today to create the next generation of programming languages.

More important than improvements in the compilers or languages themselves are the enhancements to object libraries. Libraries and frameworks are the major leverage point in object-oriented programming because you don't have to reinvent the wheel every time you program. Instead, you can inherit automatically from libraries included with your compiler or from third-party sources.

Most of the libraries out there today are foundation libraries—they supply generic components such as windows, dialog boxes, and data-management objects. Although these are important building blocks, I believe that in the next decade we'll see the emergence of an object-oriented components industry.

This industry will be a combination of today's hardware components market, where generic, off-the-shelf components compete primarily in price and performance, and the commercial library market, where packages compete based on compatibility and functionality. Ideally, generic software objects will be mass-produced so that linked-list managers, windowing systems, file managers, and so on will be so widely available that no one will ever need to write these things again. Only then can a higher-level components industry emerge to supply specialized objects for vertical market applications.

Like the application-specific integrated circuit market, these components will be more expensive, but they'll provide a competitive advantage to buyers. At that point, the software market will belong not to the "wizards" who write every piece of software from scratch but to those who can work at higher levels, solving application problems by combining existing components.

Organizations will create libraries of objects that embody the operations of their business. One can imagine an investment bank creating objects to evaluate the investment potential of startup firms. These objects might have behaviors based on the knowledge acquired from specialized neural networks or heuristics based on the work of experts. Or an insurance company might develop a library of objects for transaction processing and risk assessment. No doubt some organizations will closely guard the libraries of objects they develop, considering them to be trade secrets as important as the formula for Coca Cola. Other companies, in an attempt to recoup the large software development costs, will sell or license the libraries on the open market.

The ever-increasing cost of software development has made the library market a necessary part of our industry's economic survival. Object-oriented programming may well be the catalyst that allows us to move beyond our cottage-industry approach to an industrial revolution of software development.

Beyond Programming

Today, the most accepted way of developing software, even if you're using an object-oriented language, is primitive: You write code in a text editor, compile it, and test it. Yet we have created amazingly innovative, visual ways for our users to design machines, draw graphs, generate reports, assemble documents, and lay out newsletters. I suspect that once we've developed a sufficiently large base of object libraries, we'll need to develop higher-level tools for software development.

Already some systems, such as Asymetrix's Toolbook and the NeXTStep environment on the NeXT machine, show how we can build applications visually. These systems are limited in the range of things that can be done without programming, but they fit well with the philosophy of object-oriented programming. The goal, after all, is to reduce the software development effort.

Similarly, many programmers in the mainframe world use CASE diagramming tools to analyze and validate their designs before writing a single line of code. Some of the integrated CASE systems enable automatic code generation, though maintenance of this code is usually difficult.

For many types of software development, a visual approach with the right object-oriented methodology could help eliminate even more of the traditional programming bottleneck. When we have objects as sophisticated as the applications themselves, we shouldn't have to write reams of code to combine them into complete systems.

I'm not saying that programming will disappear; on the contrary, evidence supports the belief that programming is a growing market. The growth of programmable products (spreadsheets, databases, even word processors) and the booming market for low-end programming tools attest to this. And someone will need to program these higher-level development systems as well as create libraries of objects for visual programming.

Challenges

We will face many challenges before reaching the stage of having huge object libraries and visual tools. One of these is widespread dissemination of OOP, which requires that the skills of legions of programmers be updated. The development of easy-to-use OOP languages should make this much easier. However, I often wonder how we will ever hope to integrate object-oriented programming concepts into older languages such as Basic, COBOL, and RPG. For individual programmers, having OOP skills will be an advantage for several years. Beyond that, it will become a requirement.

One of the toughest challenges lies in creating standards for object-oriented libraries. Today, most object-oriented languages support a mechanism for persistence that enables us to store and retrieve objects to and from disk. This lets us convert object data between languages, but we must take it a step further: We must be able to use object libraries from different languages in a given programming project with full access to all functionality.

Today, it's impossible to access objects written in C++ from Turbo Pascal or vice versa. In fact, you can't access objects directly between any two object-oriented languages without some kind of conversion and loss of functionality. This barrier must be overcome before interoperability between development systems can be achieved. There's no one perfect programming language, object-oriented or otherwise, and we need to be able to select the best language for the job independent of the class libraries. Otherwise, we'll either waste our efforts converting libraries between languages or lock ourselves into single-language solutions for all applications and cripple our productivity.

The Object Management Group is working to achieve common standards between languages. However, at some stage, object management support must be present in the operating system, where it belongs, so that all languages can use a common service.

Myths of OOP

If you've discussed object-oriented programming with other programmers, you've no doubt heard some of the myths. Where they are accepted, they hinder our progress in advancing object-oriented programming.

One myth says that object-oriented programming is a single language. But remember that OOP is a philosophy, an approach that can be done in many different languages. Don't confuse the limitations of any particular language or compiler with those of OOP itself.

Another myth is that object-oriented programming is inefficient. This is something I've heard programmers use to dismiss OOP without any investigation. Object-oriented programming with hybrid languages such as C++ and Turbo Pascal proves that nothing is inherently inefficient in OOP; even the performance of older languages such as Smalltalk has improved dramatically in recent years.

You may hear traditional DOS and mainframe programmers claim that OOP is only for graphics applications. However, OOP concepts are general-purpose and apply to all programs, graphical or not.

Yet another myth says that object-oriented programming is incompatible with existing languages and libraries. Of course, one of the advantages of using a hybrid language such as C++ or Turbo Pascal is that you have complete and easy access to all your existing libraries. Even the pure object-oriented languages such as Actor let you access external libraries written in C.

The final myth of object-oriented programming is that it's just old wine in a new bottle. Perhaps, once you get past terms such as *method*, *message*, *polymorphism*, and *inheritance*, nothing is going on that can't be done in a traditional structured programming language. It is unfortunate that there are so many new terms, but make no mistake—the terms are different. A message is not the same as a function call, and inheritance is not the same as copying and pasting code.

Certainly one can mimic object-oriented programming in procedural languages (after all, that's how the earliest C++ compilers worked—by translating object-oriented code into standard C code), but the difference is one of practicality. Object-oriented programming languages provide built-in mechanisms that support encapsulation, inheritance, and polymorphism so that you can spend your time solving application problems rather than fighting with language compilers.

Going Down the Road

As you know, learning object-oriented programming is not a trivial task. Its concepts are easy—deceptively so. Applying the concepts is more difficult. To learn OOP, you must immerse yourself in objects, at least during the initial stages. Examine good OOP applications that come with your tools or are available on BBSs. And take to heart the examples Gary has presented in these pages. Build on the ideas presented here to create object-oriented games, simulations, expert systems, and business applications.

The most important piece of advice anyone can give you is to learn OOP by experimenting—first with other programmers' code or design and then with your own. If you keep your objects simple, you'll be amazed at how you can solve problems of exponentially increasing complexity with only a linear increase in effort. The key is to create objects that solve small pieces of the problem and reuse them. Then you can write your own future of object-oriented programming.

Zack Urlocker
December 1990

References
and
Resources

If you want more information about C++, Delphi, Visual Basic, dBASE for Windows, modeling, or chaos theory, the following books are worth looking into. They're only a sampling of the many works available on these subjects, but they reflect what I have on my shelves. Most of them have in some way contributed to my understanding of these tough topics.

In addition, a number of computer-related journals publish excellent articles on object-oriented programming in most issues: *AI Expert, Byte, C++ Report, dBase Informant, Delphi Informant, Dr. Dobb's Journal, Journal of Object-Oriented Programming, PC Techniques,* and *Windows Tech Journal.* I recommend all of these for up-to-date and historical information on techniques and the latest happenings in object-oriented programming.

Abraham, Ralph, and Christopher Shaw. *Dynamics: The Geometry of Behavior* (four volumes). Santa Cruz, Calif.: Aerial Press, 1984-1989.

A great introduction to and study of dynamics using pictures. If you really want to get a feeling for chaos theory, look into this one. Starts with periodic behavior and works toward the harder stuff: chaotic and bifurcation behavior. Great personalized drawings.

Casti, John L. Alternate Realities: *Mathematical Models of Nature and Man.* New York: John Wiley & Sons, 1989.

A thorough mathematical discussion of modeling. Chapters on formal representation, cellular automata, catastrophe theory, chaos, and the relationship of modeling to the way we view the world.

Eckel, Bruce. *Thinking in C++.* Prentice-Hall, Englewood Cliffs, N.J., 1995.

Not surprisingly, my favorite book on C++ programming; many pages of code, descriptions, and ideas about C++. Goes into many advanced topics I haven't covered: operator overloading, multiple inheritance, references, templates, container classes, debugging, passing objects in and out of functions, and so on. A great book to explore and study if you want to get to the heart of C++.

Ellis, Margaret, and Bjarne Stroustrup. *The Annotated C++ Reference Manual.* AT&T, 1990.

This is still the "first" word on C++ terminology and language description. If you want to know exactly how Bjarne defines C++, get a copy. Not for the faint-hearted, though, and certainly not light reading—as the title says, it's really a reference.

Entsminger, Gary L, *Developing Paradox Databases.* New York: M&T, 1993.

My introduction to developing object-based database applications using Paradox for Windows.

Entsminger, Gary L. *Secrets of the Visual Basic Masters,* 2nd ed., Indianapolis, IN, Sams, 1994.

My introduction to programming and thinking in Visual Basic.

Gleick, James. *Chaos: Making a New Science.* **New York: Viking Press, 1987.**

The already classic introduction to chaos theory. Very easy, fun reading. Focuses as much on the people who rediscovered chaos as on the theory itself. Anyone interested in chaos should start here.

Hofstadter, Douglas, and Daniel Dennett. *The Mind's I.* **New York: Bantam Books, 1981.**

Like all of Hofstadter's books, this one really gets you thinking. A collection of stories and essays about self-reflection, self-consciousness, recursion, machines with souls, scientific speculation, and other mind-stretching ideas.

Meyer, Bertrand. *Object-oriented Software Construction.* **Englewood Cliffs, N.J.: Prentice-Hall, 1988.**

A good discussion of the issues and principles of software design using object-oriented techniques. Outlines the path leading to object orientation and generally aims to convince the reader to program with objects. The second half of the book (unfortunately for C++ and Turbo Pascal programmers) focuses entirely on Meyer's language, Eiffel, making it less useful than it could have been. Worth a look, though.

Mitchell, Stephen. *Tao Te Ching.* **New York: Harper & Row, 1988.**

This is the translation of Lao-tzu's wise book that I used while writing and revising this book. Highly recommended. "The master observes the world, but trusts his inner vision. He allows things to come and go. His heart is open as the sky."

Sethi, Ravi. *Programming Languages: Concepts and Constructs.* **Reading, Mass.: Addison-Wesley, 1989.**

An excellent study of the development, design, and content of modern programming languages. Contains several fine chapters on object-oriented programming and good discussions of Modula-2, C++, and Smalltalk. Chapters on encapsulation, inheri-tance, functional programming, and logic programming and several tough, advanced chapters on interpreters and lambda calculus. Highly recommended if you're studying the development of programming languages.

Stewart, Ian. *Does God Play Dice? The Mathematics of Chaos.* New York: Basil Blackwell, 1989.

An in-depth study of the mathematics of chaos, turbulence, and strange attractors. Combines history, mathematics, and philosophy. Good discussions of logistic mapping, Lorenz and Henon attractors, and fractals.

Vasey, Phil, et al. *Prolog++ Programming Reference Manual.* London: Logic Programming Associates Ltd., 1990.

One of those rare creatures: a programming manual that really shines. In addition to showing you how to program in Prolog++, the object-oriented version of Prolog, it compares object-oriented languages and discusses the key features of OOP. Available from Quintus Computer Systems in Mountain View, Calif.

Yourdon, E.N., and L.L. Constantine. *Structured Design.* Englewood Cliffs, N.J.: Prentice-Hall, 1979.

A classic work on structured methodology by the gurus of the field.

Glossary

abstract type—A specific kind of base type designed to be used strictly as a basis for other types. It has no instances and thus can be used only to derive new types. It specifies an interface for all types derived from it. You use an abstract type to group common code. For example, if you have several collection types, they may all inherit from a single abstract type. Also known as a *formal class* in some languages.

access specifier—A keyword that controls access to data members and methods within user-defined types. C++ has three: *private*, *protected*, and *public*. *Friend* can give access to external functions. Delphi's ancestor, Turbo Pascal, had one: *private*. Delphi has three: *private*, *protected*, and *public*. (See the individual definitions for *private*, *protected*, *public*, and *friend*.)

Actor—An object-oriented language for Microsoft Windows.

ancestor—The type from which a descendant type inherits characteristics and behaviors. Also known as a *base type*.

base type—Defines a common interface to a group of descendant types. It generalizes the intended uses for a hierarchy of types. In other words, it describes the range of messages an object of a type can handle.

behavior—Another name for a method declared within a type.

binding (early)—Resolving a method call at compile time.

binding (late)—Resolving a method call at run time. When we resolve a method call, we insert the code to determine the address (or another reference) of the method definition at the point where the method is called.

browser—A software tool for inspecting object hierarchies.

built-in type—A type (such as `double` or `char`) included in a language. The compiler already knows how to handle it and doesn't have to learn about it each time it encounters an instance of one.

chaos—Stochastic (or random) behavior occurring in a deterministic system.

characteristic—Another name for data declared within a type.

class—A user-defined type in C++, Delphi & Database for Windows.

composition—Including user-defined object types as parts of other object types, as opposed to derivation (inheritance).

constructor—A special kind of method that initializes a type. In C++, a constructor has the same name as its class:

```
class Flower {
public:
  Flower();   // constructor
};
```

In C++, the compiler calls a constructor by default whenever you define an instance of a class. The constructor will be called at the point of definition or during dynamic allocation when you use the `new` operator. A user-defined type (class) can have more than one constructor, but none of them can be virtual.

In Delphi, a constructor is represented by the `Create` method.

data hiding—Removing some data from public view. Also known as *data abstraction* or *encapsulation*.

data members—Characteristics of a type.

declaration—A declaration introduces one or more names (object, function, set of functions, type, method, template, value, or label) into a program without specifying the body (the implementation) of methods. A declaration tells the compiler that data or functions exist but not where or how they're used. For example, the following are declarations in C++:

```
extern int x;
struct s;
class a;
```

These are definitions:

```
int a;
extern const c = 0;
struct s { int x; int y );
int behavior(int x) { return x + a; }
```

The following are Delphi declarations:

```
Location = class (TObject)
  Field : Integer;
  procedure Method();
end;
```

definition—A function definition looks like a declaration except that it has a body. A body is a collection of statements enclosed in braces ({}). Braces indicate the beginning and end of a block of code. In C++:

```
int behavior(int sex, int age)
{ /* Code here */ }
```

When we define a variable, we create space for it:

```
int X;
```

An example of an Delphi definition is:

```
A : Integer;
```

When we declare a variable, we tell the compiler that space exists somewhere for the variable but not how it's implemented. We can declare a variable more than once, but we can define it only once.

delete—A C++ operator that destroys a dynamic instance of an object type. It calls the destructor and then releases the memory allocated for the instance.

derivation—Another name for inheritance.

descendant—A type that inherits the characteristics and behaviors of another type. Also known as a *derived type*.

destructor—A special type of method that performs cleanup for a user-defined object type. In C++, a destructor has the same name as the class in which it's declared, preceded by a tilde:

```
class Insect {
public:
  Insect();        // constructor
  ~Insect();       // destructor
};
```

In Delphi, a destructor is represented by the Free method:

```
MyObject.Free;
```

In C++, all destructors in an inheritance hierarchy are called, not inherited. Thus, each object type that's dynamic must have its own destructor. Memory for static and automatic objects (instances of classes) is allocated and deallocated automatically by the compiler. Memory allocated for dynamic objects using the `new` operator, however, must be deallocated using the `delete` operator.

dispose—Delphi procedure for deallocating objects allocated on the heap:

```
Dispose(CirclePointer);
```

dynamic binding—Another name for late binding. See *binding (late)*.

dynamic variable allocation—A variable allocated on the heap and manipulated with pointers. Creating and destroying variables at run time instead of compile time. See *binding (late)*.

Eiffel—A completely object-oriented language available on UNIX.

encapsulation—Combining data (characteristics) with the methods (behaviors) for manipulating it; organizing code into user-defined types.

event—An occurrence that affects a program from the outside world. Examples are keystrokes, mouse-button clicks, a character from a serial port, and occurrences triggered by the system (DOS, BIOS), such as a timer tick.

expert system—Through a knowledge base of expert information, maps the input characteristics and behaviors of a system, problem, pattern, or object to a specific output system, problem, pattern, or object. Input characteristics can represent colors, sizes, processes, events, symptoms, and so on. Output represents a solution, advice, pattern match, decision, and so on.

friend—In C++, a function or method given permission to access a type (class) member. A friend can be a function or a class:

```
class SomeInfo {
int X;
public:
  friend void AFriend_function(X*, int);
                           // a friend function
  friend class AFriendClass;   // a friend class
};
```

hierarchy—A group of types derived from a base type.

hybrid language—Incorporates features of both imperative and object-oriented languages.

implementation—Describes how a user-defined type works; the interface describes how a type works. You can compile, but not link, code with just the interface description. Therefore, you can create different implementations later and link them in without recompiling the rest of the project. By separating the interface from the implementation, we isolate bugs and make experimentation easier.

inheritance—Organizing user-defined types into hierarchies.

initialization—Setting a variable or instance of a type to a specific value.

inspector—A tool for examining the data and methods of an object.

instance—A variable of a type. Also known as an *object*.

interface—In C++, the class declaration; in Delphi, the object type definition. The interface says, "Here's what a type looks like, and here are its behaviors," but it doesn't specify how the type behaves; that's left to the implementation. The interface describes what a type does, whereas the implementation describes how the type works.

member functions—In C++, another name for *methods*. Throughout this book we use *methods* as the generic term for the behaviors declared within a type.

message—The name of a method passed to an instance of an object type. When you send a message to an instance of an object, you call one of its methods. To send a message to an instance of an object, you specify the object and the method you want to invoke. For example, if AType is an instance of an object and Init is a method, the following code sends an Init message to the object. In C++:

```
AType.Init();
```

In Delphi:

```
AType.Init;
```

method—In C++, a function declared within a class and used to access the data within the class. Also called a *member function*. In Delphi, a procedure or function declared within an object and used to access the data within the object.

model—A mathematical representation of some aspect of the world.

new—An operator (in C++) or procedure (in Delphi) for allocating space for a type on the heap and initializing the object in one operation. In C++, new is invoked with a constructor call:

```
Circle *ACircle = new Circle(30,30,30);
```

object—In object-oriented programming, an instance of a class (an object type); a record (data and methods) that can inherit.

Objective-C—An object-oriented language that combines C and Smalltalk.

override—Reimplement, redefine. Used to describe the reimplementation of methods by object types.

pointer—Contains the address of a variable. In C++, designated by "*":

```
int *intPointer;
```

In Delphi, the pointer is designated by "^":

```
IntPointer  = ^Integer;
```

polymorphic type—A type that's not known until run time.

polymorphism—Single interface, many implementations. Specifically, calling a virtual method for a variable whose precise type isn't known at compile time. The behavior is established at run time via late binding.

private—In C++, any members following `private` can be accessed only by methods declared within the same class. In Delphi, any members following `private` can be accessed only by functions within the same unit.

protected—In C++, any members following `protected` can only be accessed only by member functions within the same class or by member functions of classes derived from this class.

public—In C++ and Delphi, means "anyone can use it." Any members (methods or data) following `public` can be accessed without restriction.

scope—The lifetime and accessibility of a variable. Defines which parts of a program can access specific variables. For example, a variable declared within a function is local by default and can be accessed only by code within the function.

Smalltalk—One of the earliest object-oriented languages. Developed by Xerox Palo Alto Research Center in the 1970s.

static instance—An instance of an object type named in the `var` declaration (in Delphi) and allocated in the data segment and on the stack. In C++, static instances have global lifetimes and are initialized before `main()` and cleaned up after `main()`.

static method—A method resolved by the compiler at compile time. See *early binding*.

strange attractor—In phase space, an attractor is a point or limit cycle in a dynamic system that draws or attracts a system. In other words, as the system changes state, it can reach equilibrium (settle down) to a point or a cycle. A strange attractor is one that's broken up or fragmented in phase space. It represents a system whose order, when plotted in a time series, isn't obvious but shows itself in a shape (an order) in phase space.

strong vs. weak type checking—A strong type-checking system accepts only those expressions that it can guarantee to be correct. A weak type-checking system will allow potentially unsafe expressions to pass through the compiler.

structured programming—Combines two ideas: structured program flow (the flow of control of a program is determined by the syntax of the program code) and invariants (assertions that hold every time control reaches them).

type—The type of a variable tells us the range of values (or states) it can assume and the operators we can apply to it. Type is everything we can know about a class of objects that a variable or instance can represent.

type extensibility—The ability to add functionality to code. You derive new types (through inheritance) and add or modify behaviors and characteristics to suit your needs.

unit—In Delphi, a collection of constants, data types, variables, procedures, and functions that are compiled separately. If data members in a type are declared after the keyword `private`, any function, method, or procedure within a unit can access them but nothing outside the unit can.

user-defined type—A single structure containing the characteristics and behaviors for the type. In C++, Delphi, and dBASE for Windows, we call a user-defined type a *class*. The compiler treats it as a built-in type. Throughout this book, *class*, *user-defined type* and *object type* are often used interchangeably.

virtual method—A method resolved by the compiler at run time. See *late binding*. In C++, you declare a virtual method by preceding the method name with the keyword `virtual`:

```
virtual void Show();
```

In Delphi, you declare a virtual method by adding the keyword virtual after the method:

```
procedure Show; virtual;
```

virtual method table—In Delphi, each type (object) has a VMT that contains information about the type, including its size and a pointer to the code implementing each of its virtual methods. When an instance of a type sends a message to a constructor, the constructor establishes a link to the VMT automatically.

Each type has one VMT; each instance of a type links to the type VMT.

The C++ equivalent of the VMT is called a *VTABLE*. The pointer that points to the VTABLE is called the *VPTR*.

with—Delphi keyword. You can access a type's data members by using a dot (for example, `AType.Member`) or a `with` statement:

```
with AType do
begin
   X:= 2;
   Y:= 3;
   Z:= 4;
end;
```

Index

W

X